Muslims:

5 Biblical Essentials Every Christian Must Know and Do

Renod Bejjani

WestBow Press books may be ordered through booksellers or by contacting:

WestBow Press
A Division of Thomas Nelson & Zondervan
1663 Liberty Drive
Bloomington, IN 47403
www.westbowpress.com
1 (866) 928-1240

ISBN: 978-1-9736-6297-6 (sc)
ISBN: 978-1-9736-6296-9 (e)

Library of Congress Control Number: 2019905942

Print information available on the last page.

WestBow Press rev. date: 06/04/2019

Contents

CHAPTER 1

The Problem, the Solution, and You

I was born in an Arabic Islamic country in 1963 and spent my childhood in the Middle East and North Africa (MENA). As a Christian growing up in a region where 99 percent of the population professed to be Muslim, incredibly early in life I experienced what it meant to be persecuted for one's faith. By persecution, I don't mean that I was called names—although that happened more times than I can count. The persecution I endured began at an early age and included beatings, sexual assaults, threats on my life, and even being kidnapped. I experienced so much hatred because of my faith in the region where Christianity—a religion founded on God's great *love*—was born two thousand years ago.

The MENA region, although Muslim now, was "Christianized" by AD 600. Around 50 percent[1] of the population in MENA was Christian by the fourth century. Christianity continued to grow until it became the dominant religion of the entire Mediterranean world. Christianity even spread throughout the Persian Gulf region into modern-day Arabia, Iran, and Yemen.[2] Today, Islam dominates that area.

---

[1] "The Rise of Christianity," *Historical Atlas of the Mediterranean,* Accessed Oct. 11, 2018, http://explorethemed.com/christian.asp?c=1.

[2] John Phillip Jenkins, *The Lost History of Christianity: The Thousand-Year Golden Age of the Church in the Middle East, Africa and Asia—and How it Died.* (New York: Harper-Collins, 2008), 12.

Have you ever wondered why the birthplace of the Christian faith is now almost all Islamic? While you are considering that question, let me ask another: Have you noticed a rise in the Muslim faith in your country?

Today, the same shift from Christianity to Islam that occurred in MENA is happening in Christianized nations worldwide. And unless these historical trends change, it is not a matter of *if* but *when* Islam will become the predominant religion in your nation.

The Wrong Assumption

Many people wrongly assume the reason Christianity has almost vanished from MENA is because evangelism and conversion to Christianity is typically illegal and dangerous in Islamic nations. But just like it is today in MENA, so it was two thousand years ago: spreading the Christian faith or converting to Christianity were and are often punishable, sometimes by torture and even by death. The New Testament gives us a glimpse into the various persecutions those spreading the Christian faith endured: being imprisoned, death threats, whippings (lashings), beatings, and death by the sword and by stoning. Historical records report that Jesus's own disciples suffered horrific deaths due to spreading the Christian faith. Peter, Andrew, and Philip were crucified; Matthew and James were stoned; Thomas was speared; Bartholomew was skinned alive and beheaded.[3] Other Christians also were killed in horrific ways, such as by being burned alive and by being fed to starving wild animals like lions in sports arenas.[4]

Yes, Christians in Islamic countries today are experiencing very real persecution, and so did Christians during the first three hundred years after Christ's ascension to heaven. Knowing what they would face, Jesus told His followers to tell others about Him.

---

[3] Joyce E. Salisbury, *The Blood of Martyrs, Unintended Consequences of Ancient Violence.* (Rutledge: New York, 2004), 3.

[4] Ibid.

Then Jesus came to them and said, "All authority in heaven and on earth has been given to me. Therefore go and make disciples of all nations, baptizing them in the name of the Father and of the Son and of the Holy Spirit, and teaching them to obey everything I have commanded you. And surely, I am with you always, to the very end of the age." (Matt. 28:18–20 NIV)

Jesus knew the task He had given His followers seemed impossible. He also knew that obedience to His commands would lead to their persecution and even death. To help them, He equipped His followers with the Holy Spirit and gave them specific instructions that outlined how to successfully complete the job He had given them.

Despite the dangers and intense persecution Jesus's followers faced in the first few centuries, they persisted in their faithful obedience to these principles. As a result, Christianity spread rapidly, and the church prevailed over the mighty Roman Empire. By AD 600, MENA was Christianized. Yet today, this region is almost completely Muslim.

The Solution and You

One of the reasons I wrote this book is to make you aware of the global trend toward Islam and the problematic implications that reality would have on all our futures. More importantly, I want to help you understand the solution to the Islamic problem. I have found that there are five biblical essentials that every Christian must know and do. Throughout history, whenever and wherever Christians have followed these five principles, Christianity has grown—and other religions have diminished. Whenever and wherever Christians have not done these five things, Christianity has decreased while Islam increased.

I wrote this book to help you do the following:

1. Become aware of and understand the problem created by the Christian response to Muslims and the devastating impact that creates globally.

2. Realize how the majority of Christians (perhaps even you) have unknowingly contributed to the problem.
3. Discover God's primary purposes for your life.
4. Understand and use the five biblical essentials to live out God's purposes for your life. These principles were created by God and are the most effective means of solving the global problem.

My hope is that you will experience the perfect joy that comes from living out God's primary purpose for your life and that you will become intentional about being part of the solution and making the world better for all of us today—and for future generations.

Growing Up among Muslims

I grew up knowing who Jesus is, and still, for the first forty-five years of my life, I felt as if something was missing. I sensed that I was not fulfilling God's primary purpose for my life, but I wasn't sure what that really meant. Like many Christians, I was unaware of the problem the Christian response to Muslims poses for our world. God changed all that around 2008. The following story is a brief explanation of how God helped me understand my purpose as a Christian as well as revealing the global problem and why I needed to be part of the solution.

My Christian-Lebanese parents married when they were sixteen and eighteen years old. My father had dropped out of school at fourteen to help support his family. He worked in construction, and after my parents married, they left Lebanon and lived wherever my father could find work—which meant they were moving from one Islamic nation to the next.

I was born in Iraq in 1963. For most of my childhood, we lived in a country where the population was 90 percent Muslim and 10 percent Christian—a country that had been predominately Christian fourteen hundred years earlier. Today, it's estimated that only less than 1 percent of the population of Iraq is still Christian, and over 99 percent is now Muslim.[5]

Even though we lived in a Muslim culture, my mom wanted to make sure I grew up as a Christian. Every day she read the Bible to me, taught me Christian songs, and prayed with me. She also took me to a church that had a charismatic preacher. I was in awe of that preacher and the passionate way he shared the gospel. I was so impressed that I tried to imitate him. When I was four years old, I would stand in front of our home and "preach" as loudly as I could. I do not remember the words, but I think I repeated things I heard in church or that my mom had read to me from the Bible. I was not intentionally trying to share the gospel; I was a child imitating an adult who had made an inspirational impression on me. Whatever words I said, I tried to speak with as much enthusiasm as our preacher at church did.

One evening I was "preaching" in front of our home while my parents were inside preparing dinner. Suddenly, a man grabbed hold of me, covered my mouth so I couldn't scream, and abducted me. In the darkness, he took me to the rooftop of a building and tortured me. After repeatedly abusing me, he picked me up and held me upside down by one ankle and dangled me over the side of the building, acting as if he was about to drop me to my death.

He shook me and whispered angry words at me so he would not be heard by the neighbors. I have no idea how long he held me there; it felt like eternity. Inexplicably, he then got very still and quiet. I do not know what changed his mind and kept him from killing me—but he pulled me back in, tied me up, and left me on the rooftop of that building. After much struggle, I eventually freed myself and found my way home. I still remember the chaotic scene I found when I stumbled through the doorway to my house that night. Friends and neighbors had gathered, and my mother, understandably, was crying hysterically, pleading for someone to find her missing son.

As a four-year-old, I did not understand the evil things that man

[5] Jenkins, *The Lost History*, 152.

had done to me. I did not understand why he had kidnapped and hurt me or what I may have done to deserve it. The only thing I really understood was that he hated me—and he wasn't the only one.

When we later moved to North Africa, we lived in Libya. The country was Christianized through 640 AD[6] but now has only one hundred thousand Christians living in it (mainly non-Libyans); 97 percent of the population in Libya is Muslim.[7] In Libya, I continued to go out in front of our home wherever we lived and preach as loudly as I could—which didn't make me any friends. In fact, I was attacked, beaten, and sexually assaulted on at least eight separate occasions by different Muslim men. As they abused me, they called me "*kafir*."

I Hated Muslims

As a child, I simply associated being tortured with being called kafir. It wasn't until I was eleven years old that I learned that kafir, which is sometimes translated as "infidel" in English, means "unbeliever." It is used the way a Christian might use the word *pagan* to refer to an unbeliever who is polytheistic or worships more than the one true God. To these Muslim men, I was an infidel, a kafir, because I did not believe in the God of Islam. Finally, I understood that Muslims (at least those who had attacked me through the years) viewed me as a blasphemous kafir, deserving of torture, even death. As you can imagine, I grew to fear Muslims and became incredibly angry with them, even hating them. I viewed Muslims as my enemies and as the enemies of Christianity.

My rage against Muslims intensified in April 1975 while I was living in a Muslim part of Beirut. That's when the Lebanese Civil War began. Miraculously, I survived the extreme dangers of being a Christian "enemy" in the war between Christians and Muslims.

---

[6] Ibid.

[7] Ronald Bruce St. John, *Historical Dictionary of Libya*, Third Edition. (The Scarecrow Press Inc: Lanham, MD, 1998), 998, 287.

But as I watched the guerilla street warfare around me, my hatred for Muslims grew.

I Hated God

In September of 1976, at the age of thirteen, I traveled alone to the United States of America as an international student and a first-generation immigrant.

As you can imagine, I was a troubled young man. By age eighteen, I had transferred my rage from Muslims toward God. I doubted God's existence. I reasoned that if God were real, He would not allow all that killing to be justified in His name by Muslims and Christians alike.

I also reasoned that if Christ were real, He would have protected me against the horrors I experienced during the first thirteen years of my life. To me, it seemed that all these evil things had happened to me because I was associated with Christ.

So, I left God and turned to a rebellious and sinful lifestyle. My prodigal ways lasted around twenty-five years.

But God never hated me. He never left me.

God is love, and He redeemed me. The story of how God did it is epic but not the subject of this book. Suffice it to say that God knew my heart was broken and that my soul was in desperate need. He took me back to the country of my youth and showed me that I was not alone in my pain or heartache—that I wasn't alone in my need for Him. He showed me that entire nations of people were lost without Him. Amid it all, He taught me to love my enemies.

What to Do with Muslims Extremists and Conflicts

On Tuesday, September 11, 2001, at around 6:45 a.m., I was preparing breakfast for my children in our California home. What had begun as a normal morning abruptly spun into chaos when my children came running into the kitchen, screaming in terror. I could not understand exactly why they were so frightened, but they grabbed me by the hands and dragged me to the living room, where I watched television news reports of the Islamic terrorists' attacks on America.

As I watched the Twin Towers of the World Trade Center collapse, all the anger, rage, and hatred I had felt toward Muslims in the past reawakened within me. I knew the Bible taught to love and pray for everyone—including our enemies—and I still viewed Muslims as the enemy of Christianity and by extension, most Christianized nations. Even though God had already redeemed me and had set me on a healing path that included becoming part of the solution to the Islamic problem, the horror of the next few hours reminded me of the fear, hurt, and anger I had experienced throughout my childhood and young adult years.

For so many years, my view of Muslims mirrored that of the Christians I knew worldwide. I had acted indifferently toward Muslims and stayed away from them whenever possible. And when terrorism in the name of Islam became a reality for people worldwide with the attacks of 9/11, like most Christians, I felt angry with Muslims. I understood the hate, confusion, and fear people displayed toward Muslims—because I had felt all those things myself.

After the 9/11 attacks, Christians and non-Christians who knew I had grown up in MENA and knew about the work I was doing with Muslims asked me to help them understand or try to make sense of the horrific events. They asked questions like these:

- What is radical Islam?
- Why do Muslims want to harm us?
- What should we do about Muslims in my area, my nation, and the world?
- Should we allow Muslims, refugees or otherwise, to come here?
- How can we protect ourselves, our freedoms, and our way of life?
- How do the Arab/Israeli conflict and Islamic wars in the rest of the world affect me, my loved ones, and future generations?

I continue to hear questions like these daily. You may have similar questions of your own. All these questions, above or otherwise, could typically be summarized into one: What do we do with and about Muslims?

Problem, Solution, and Me

Prior to the attacks in 2001, God had begun the process of healing and changing my heart. But that year I began to understand that the same things that had happened in MENA to turn it from Christianized to up to 99 percent Muslim are happening in currently Christianized nations, including the United States. I saw how the majority of Christians were unknowingly contributing to this alarming trend.

I wanted to be part of the solution to turn the trend around. In response to what God was teaching me, I read hundreds of books, attended dozens of conferences, and met, saw, studied, and learned from hundreds of Christian leaders, experts, organizations, and ordinary believers who were actively working to reverse this trend locally and globally. I wholeheartedly applied what I learned. Unfortunately, most of it was ineffective.

The Least Effective Majority

Most well-meaning Christians who are trying to reverse the alarming trend toward Islam are part of what I call the least effective majority (LEM). For about seven years, I was part of the LEM and saw little, if any, impact. Frustrated, I began to closely examine the teachings and the results of the LEM.

I saw that only a few of their methods produced satisfactory results, but only in certain areas and only for a relatively brief period of time. Their methodologies were academic, ineffective, difficult, complicated, unsustainable, not duplicable, and not applicable in most places—locally or globally, Islamic or Christianized; moreover, I felt overwhelmed, as do many Christians who want to be part of the solution. It seemed as if I needed to have doctorate degrees to understand and take part in these methods.

I now understand that the reason I, along with the rest of the LEM, were not successful is because we did not use the five biblical essentials you'll learn about in this book.

The Most Effective Minority

In contrast, I noticed that a minority of believers who were working toward a solution were consistently well received and effective in both Christianized and Islamic nations. I refer to this group as the most effective minority (MEM). I examined their methods and saw a common thread: five God-given principles that are God-dependent, simple, duplicable, doable, workable, sustainable, effective, and fruitful. When I personally applied these five biblical essentials, I saw that they produced successful results in Christianized and Islamic nations. Because these principles work so well, I began teaching them to others and have seen their consistent effectiveness both locally and globally.

Changing the World

By 2011, it became clear to me that most churches and Christians worldwide were not part of the solution; rather, by their inaction, they were part of the problem. Although Christians in the Westernized countries have a greater awareness of Muslims now than they did in 2001, not much has improved. The trend toward Islam continues across MENA and in other traditionally Christian parts of the world. To reverse this trend and change the world to make it better (especially for future generations), more Christians and churches must become aware and involved. While those in the MEM are mighty, they are small in number. Significant change will happen when we decrease the numbers in the LEM category and increase the numbers of Christians relying on and using the most effective practices. The goal is to make

MEM stand for the most effective *majority*. In other words, we need more world changers.

For twelve years prior to 2011, I had the feeling that God wanted me to do more in leading churches and Christians to be part of the solution, but I did not tell anyone. During that time, hundreds of Christians told me they believed that God equipped me to do more; still, I wrestled with God, asking, "Who am I to inspire others to get involved and to equip them for the task?" Eventually, God gave the same answer He gives to everyone who answers His call: *"It is not about who you are, it is all about who I Am."* I simply needed to remember that my job was to allow the one and only God to use me to fulfill His purpose—to make His kingdom come and His will be done.

God showed me how He had uniquely prepared me all my life for this time in history, for this specific task. God gave me reassurance that there were countless Christians willing and able to do their part to change the world. They just needed to become aware of the problem and the solution.

So in May 2011, my amazing wife, Karen, and I took a giant leap of faith and started iHope Ministries, where I serve as president. The nonprofit ministry was the beginning of our mission answering God's call to action.

A Movement Begins

By September 11, 2012, Karen and I were ready for the next step, and we scheduled our first workshop. Our goal was to inspire and empower Christians to live out God's primary purposes for their lives by being part of the solution to change the world.

Since this was a new ministry and I was unknown in our area, we thought we would be lucky to have ten people come to that first workshop. We would have considered that an enormous success.

God overwhelmed us when 106 people showed up for the workshop! They packed into the small facility we had rented until we had standing room only. People were eager to know what to do about Muslims and how to wisely process the plethora of thoughts and emotions they were experiencing about Muslims. At the end of the event, most of those who came told us that we had given them biblical answers from a new, godly perspective—answers and a perspective they had not heard before.

That first workshop was a bigger success than we had imagined, and it sparked a movement to help change the world. On September 11, 2012, we began as a completely unknown entity. Since then, we have inspired and empowered thousands of believers to be part of the solution regarding Muslims.

In this book, I will share with you the things we teach and share at iHOPE workshops. I will share with you challenging yet inspiring stories that reveal the five essentials every Christian must know and do and illustrate how to apply these principles in your everyday life.

The Key

The five essentials work together like five grooves of a key. And like a key, if you add more grooves or take away grooves, the key will not work. The teachings of the LEM do exactly that: taking away one or more of the five essentials and adding much more complicated, difficult, and needless grooves. The five essentials are completely God-centered, God-dependent, God-trusting, and God-glorifying, and thus they consistently accomplish God's purposes.

Thousands of alumni who have been inspired and equipped by iHOPE Ministries have shared with us that this was the first time they became aware of these things and joined the movement to do their part to help change the world. They also urged me to get this "life- and world-changing" information to you.

The topic of this book may seem heavy, controversial, and uncomfortable for you. I understand that discomfort because I have felt it myself. I encourage you to push past that discomfort and to use these principles. Now, more than ever before, we need to be intentional about fulfilling God's purpose for our lives.

With that in mind, I urge you to pray as you read this book. Take time to pray right now. Release any anxiety to God. Ask Him to open your eyes, mind, and heart to see, discover, and understand His perspectives and to obey His truths.

God is calling you to join Him in His work. The world needs every Christian to do their tiny part. You can be part of the solution and make the world a better place for us, our children, and future generations.

CHAPTER 2
The Root of the Issue

Sara[8] was born and raised in a devout Muslim family in an Islamic country. She has long black hair and beautiful caramel-colored skin. Whenever she left her home, she wore a full *burqa*, a garment worn by some Muslim women to cover the entire body and face except the eyes.

As a good Muslim girl, Sara worked hard to please Allah (the Arabic word for God) and her parents. She even memorized the Quran (Islam's holy book). At one point in her youth, Sara entered a competition and placed second in reciting the Quran from memory.

As a teenager, Sara, like many Muslims do, began feeling tremendous stress about Judgment Day. She worried about whether she had performed enough good works to outweigh her faults and failings so Allah would judge her worthy of acceptance into paradise. Initially, Sara was pleased with having earned second place in the youth competition, but as she grew older, she felt intense pressure to place first in everything. Anything less, she reasoned, would displease Allah and her parents.

The Pilgrimage to Mecca

When she was twelve years old, Sara went with her father on the *Hajj* (pilgrimage) to Mecca (in Saudi Arabia). All Muslims who are able

---

[8] All names in the stories shared have been changed to protect the privacy of individuals.

are required to make the Hajj at least once in their lives. On that trip, Sara became a young *Hajji*, which is a title of honor given to a Muslim female who has successfully completed the Hajj.

As Sara and her father were on the road during the Hajj trip, they noticed a large crowd gathering. Curious, they joined the crowd to see what was happening. The crowd formed a giant circle surrounding a woman standing alone in the center. The woman was dressed in a full burqa, so no one saw her face.

Then a man walked up to the woman, drew a large and shiny sword, and beheaded the woman.

Young Sara was horrified.

Sara was told that the woman had been convicted of adultery. Under Sharia law (Islamic law), a person convicted of certain crimes, including adultery, can be executed.

Seeing that beheading motivated Sara to become an even better Muslim. Since Islam offers no assurance of salvation, Sara, like other devout Muslims, wanted to do whatever she could to please Allah to be able to enter paradise. Sara viewed Sharia law as coming from Allah and wanted to obey it completely.

Although she lived in a predominately Islamic country, Sara met a few Christians who lived there, but none of these Christians befriended her, nor did they ever share their faith in Jesus Christ as Lord and Savior with her.

Sara's New Country

Sara was seventeen years old when war erupted in her Islamic country. She became a refugee and moved with her family to a part of the United States that's often referred to as the Bible Belt. Unlike in her home country, she now lived in a place where there were many evangelical Christians and where there seemed to be a church on every street corner.

For eight years, Sara drove by churches daily. Like many Muslims, she always wondered what it was like inside a church. She was curious about what Christians did in there. Sara thought that because she was a Muslim, she would need a special invitation by a Christian to go into a church. Sara said she would have eagerly accepted, but no one invited her.

Curious about Easter and Christmas

Like many Muslims who come to Western countries, Sara did not understand Easter. She thought Christians practiced idolatry by going to church on Easter. *What does the Easter Bunny have to do with their faith? Do they worship it?* she wondered. Sara was also confused about Easter egg hunts and eggs—whether colored, plastic, or chocolate—not knowing what any of that had to do with Christianity.

Like many Muslims, Sara was also curious about Christmas and everything related to it. She thought Christians practiced more idolatry by going to church on Christmas to worship Santa Claus, this seemingly eternal being that comes out once a year and is everywhere at the same time during Christmas Eve. She was also disturbed that "Christians" celebrated this holiday by getting drunk (forbidden in Islam) around Christmas.

Fears of "Christian Immorality"

Having witnessed the beheading of an adulteress, imagine the horror Sara must have felt when she heard about "immoral Christians" getting drunk on New Year's Eve and then committing sexual sins punishable even unto death under Islamic law. Like most Muslims, Sara did not separate a person's country and religion; for example, most Muslims believe Western nations are Christian, and therefore all citizens of these nations are also Christian. So when a person in a Western country, whether an average person or a celebrity, openly engaged in sex outside of marriage, Sara saw that person as a "Christian" promoting such sins. Like many Muslims, Sara concluded that most Christians live immoral, sinful lifestyles. And like many

Muslims, Sara was fearful of being influenced by a "Christian" culture into an immoral lifestyle that would land her in hell on Judgment Day.

Unanswered Questions about Christianity

Sara, however, saw a few Christians who seemed good and moral. Like many Muslims, Sara had so many questions related to Christians and the Western lifestyle she saw every day. She desperately wanted to ask Christians, at least the seemingly moral ones, about their religion, holidays, and practices; however, Sara, a foreigner in a strange culture, was too afraid to initiate contact.

Sara knew that many of her neighbors and coworkers were Christians, but she believed they did not like her because she was Muslim; otherwise, surely one of them would have befriended her and invited her to church. Worse than the confusion and loneliness she endured, she also felt *hated*. Whenever she when out in public, it seemed as if all eyes—many of them angry—were on her.

As a Muslim, Sara did experience one unique advantage when she went shopping dressed in her burqa. Whatever aisle Sara went on in the store, it was like the parting of the sea of people in front and behind her. Long lines at checkout registers disappeared in front of her as people typically avoided her. With Islamic terrorism dominating news headlines, Sara assumed some of those shoppers were afraid that she was hiding a bomb under her burqa.

Finally, a Christian Friend

After eight years of the emotional pain of being separated from her friends and extended family, Sara learned that her favorite person in the world, her beloved grandfather, was coming from the Middle East to visit with her and her family. Her joy quickly and unexpectedly turned into overwhelming sadness when her grandfather suddenly fell ill and died within a few days of arriving in the United States.

His death prompted her to wonder, as many Muslims do when a

loved one dies, whether Allah would allow her dear grandfather into paradise. Her uncertainty overwhelmed her with worry, anxiety, and depression.

On the first day back to work after her grandfather's death, she was visibly sad. At one point, so overwhelmed by her emotions, she began to cry uncontrollably.

Jane, one of Sara's coworkers, saw her crying. Jane had always wanted to get to know Sara, but she was too afraid to approach her. Jane thought, *What would I say to a Muslim woman?* Like many Western Christians, Jane did not want to say or "do the wrong thing"; she did not want to offend Sara. And because she did not know anything about Islam, the Quran, Muslims, their history, or their culture, Jane felt inadequate. She worried, *What if Sara wants to talk religion or politics?* Jane didn't think she had anything in common with Sara, and she had no idea how to start a conversation with a shy, devout Muslim woman. (Although Sara did not wear a full burqa to work, she did wear a *hijab,* a veil that covered her hair, head, and neck and clearly identified her as a Muslim.)

That morning, moved with compassion for Sara, Jane decided to risk any awkwardness and start a conversation. She asked Sara what was wrong, but Sara could not stop crying long enough to answer. Without thinking or further analyzing the situation, Jane acted from the heart and hugged Sara.

The embrace was met with a fountain of tears falling on Jane's shoulders. At the time, Sara could not describe her thoughts and feeling about Jane's hug other than it was quite different and unlike any hug Sara had ever received; meanwhile, Jane felt emboldened by Sara's acceptance of her hug, so again without thinking or further analyzing the situation, Jane asked, "Would you like to come to church with me? When I am troubled, I find peace there. We can go Sunday morning, and then after church we can have lunch and go shopping at the mall."

Amid the sorrow and anxiety she felt, a dim spark of happiness lit in Sara's heart. *Finally!* she thought. *After eight years of being in*

America, a Christian has shown interest in me. I can't believe I get to go to a church and see what it's like.

Sara accepted Jane's invitation.

A Hijab in a Church

On Sunday morning, Sara was afraid of going to church. She wondered how Christians would respond to a Muslim woman dressed in a hijab coming into their church. To Sara's surprise, everyone in that church warmly welcomed her.

Just after Sara sat down, a man stood up on the stage and read, "The Spirit of the Lord is upon me, because he has anointed me to proclaim good news to the poor. He has sent me to proclaim liberty to the captives and recovering of sight to the blind, to set at liberty those who are oppressed, to proclaim the year of the Lord's favor. And he rolled up the scroll and gave it back to the attendant and sat down. And the eyes of all in the synagogue were fixed on him. And he began to say to them, Today, this Scripture has been fulfilled in your hearing."

Sara asked Jane, "What book did that man just read from?"

A New Follower of Christ

Jane told Sara it was from the Bible, Luke 4:18–21. Sara had many questions after church. Feeling inadequate to the task of answering Sara's deep religious questions, Jane bought a study Bible as a gift for Sara from the mall that morning.

Their friendship grew as Jane loved on Sara, prayed with her in Jesus's name, and studied the Bible with her when Sara requested it; meanwhile, Sara secretly studied the Bible daily in her Muslim home. Around eighteen months after that first hug from Jane, Sara accepted Jesus Christ as her Lord and Savior and was baptized as a follower of Christ. Since then, Sara has been living out God's primary purposes, doing her part to help change the world.

The Root Problem

Sara's story reveals why, in many nations worldwide—including the United States—Christianity is declining while Islam is rising.[9], [10] Let us begin to look into it.

Islam is the number two religion in the world today. As of 2017, there are an estimated 1.68 billion Muslims worldwide, or 23.1 percent of the world's population. And 84.7 percent of Muslims—that's around 1.43 billion Muslims—are "unreached."[11] Unreached means someone who has never heard the good news about Jesus Christ as the one-and-only Lord and Savior. Imagine *1.43 billion* people! That is an unfathomable number of people who have not been given the opportunity to know Jesus as their Savior.

God loves every single Muslim. But there are 1.43 billion loved-but-unsaved Muslims because they have not been told, "God so loved the world, that He gave His only begotten Son, that whoever believes in Him should not perish, but have everlasting life" (John 3:16 NKJV). That is the root of Christianity's Islamic problem.

Like Sara before Jane reached out to her, Muslims do not know that God made this promise: "If you confess with your mouth that Jesus is Lord and believe in your heart that God raised him from the dead, you will be saved" (Romans 10:9 ESV). They do not know they can be reconciled back to God only through Jesus: "Jesus said to him, 'I am the way, and the truth, and the life. No one comes to the Father except through me" (John 14:6 NIV).

Most Muslims who live in any of the fifty-seven predominantly

---

[9] *America's Changing Religious Landscape*. Pew Research Center. May 12, 2015. http://www.pewforum.org/2015/12/americas-changing-religious-landscape/.

[10] Michael Linka and Condrad Hacket. *Why Muslims are the World's Fastest Growing Religious Group*. Pew Research Center, April 6, 2017, http://www.pewresearch.org/fact-tank/2015/04/23/why-muslims-are-the-worlds-fastest-growing-religious-group/.

[11] *Lists:AllReligions*.JoshuaProject.AssessedOct.11,2018.https://joshuaproject.net/global/religions.

Islamic countries worldwide do not know the good news because Christians who live there typically do not share it. I did not until God convicted me.

Muslims who move to non-Islamic nations, like Sara, do not know the truth about Jesus Christ because Christians in Christianized nations do not typically try to befriend them, much less share the gospel with them. For about seven years after God redeemed me, I still did not befriend or share the good news with Muslims. Unfortunately, that kind of behavior is common.

A Growing Problem

Islamic religious beliefs, along with ongoing inaction by Christians to engage Muslims with the good news of Christ, combine to fuel the exponential growth of various problems.

Regarding Islamic religious beliefs, instead of knowing that Jesus is the only way to paradise, Muslims believe they must please God so that, in His mercy, He will allow them into heaven on Judgment Day. But Muslims do not believe salvation is guaranteed.

Islam is a religious way of life that has daily reminders to Muslims that their lives are to be God-centered, and that their ultimate destination is either heaven or hell. Where God sends them on Judgment Day depends on the good works they have done in this life. So most Muslims, just like Sara did, work hard to please God with their good works.

Most Muslims, at some point in their lives, worry and stress about whether their good works are enough to help get them into paradise. Because of all that concern, a small percentage of Muslims go to extreme measures to do things now, before it is too late, that they think please Allah. This is their way of increasing their chances of entering paradise. The world knows this small percentage as Islamic radicals, or a variation of that name.

Some Islamic radicals believe that martyrdom in a military-style fight provides the only guaranteed entrance into paradise. This minority thinks that from Allah's perspective, a military *jihad* (jihad means "struggle") is justified when it is against infidels (non-believers in their version of the god of Islam) who refuse to repent and believe in Islam; therefore, this minority is willing to commit terroristic acts (jihad, in their twisted minds) against unrepentant infidels to the extent of being martyred in the process.

Christianity's Role in the Growing Problem

Christianity has not offered a different view to 84.7 percent of the Muslims in the world[12] today who are like Sara—kind, family-oriented, and doing their best to please God. Because they have not heard that Jesus is the only way into heaven, and with Him salvation is guaranteed, 1.43 billion Muslims are working hard—futilely—to earn an unguaranteed chance into paradise.

In the meantime, a minority of Muslims who are Islamic radicals terrorize the world as they try to guarantee their own and their followers' entrance into paradise through military jihad. You have probably seen an increased number of news reports about terrorism from these Islamic radicals. And you have probably noticed (particularly on social media) the rising anger, fear, and confusion exhibited by of the rest of the world toward Muslims because of the acts of these extremists; indeed, a growing number of people worldwide (Christians and non-Christians alike) keep away from all Muslims, including the peaceful majority who are like Sara.

Fear and confusion perpetuate the inaction of Christians to engage Muslims with the good news about Jesus as Lord and Savior. As a result, Islam is growing with little, if any, resistance. It is estimated that around 10 percent of Muslims have the propensity to become

---

[12] "Lists: All Religions," *Joshua Project,* Accessed Oct. 11, 2018, https://joshuaproject.net/global/religions. https://joshuaproject.net/global/religions.

radical.[13] It is my belief that this percentage has been constant through the ages and likely will remain the same in the future. So as Islam grows worldwide—at twice the rate of Christianity[14]—the number of Islamic radicals and terroristic acts also increases.

Our true Islamic problem is that Christians, for the most part, have not offered Muslims an alternative belief system by sharing with them the good news about Jesus Christ as Lord and Savior. Not fulfilling God's primary purposes for us—*to know Him and make Him known*—is a major contributing factor to a rapidly growing Islamic problem that is creating ever-increasing terror and chaos.

You, like many Christians, may have different ideas about what contributes to or constitutes the actual Islamic problem. You may be thinking in terms of politics, military issues, social problems, terrorism, Arab/Israeli conflict, or Muslims being allowed to enter your country or city. We will cover all those issues in this book. To be sure, understanding Muslims and what our Christian response should be toward them is a complex issue—one we would be wise to view from God's perspective as revealed in the Bible. That's exactly what we will begin to do in the next chapter.

---

[13] *The World's Muslims: Religion, Politics and Society. Pew Research Center,* April 30, 2013, http://www.pewforum.org/2013/04/30/the-worlds-muslims-religion-politics-society-overview/#extremism-widely-rejected.

[14] Michael Lipka and Conrad Hacket, "Why Muslims are the world's fastest-growing religious group," *Pew Research Center,* April 6, 2017, http://www.pewresearch.org/fact-tank/2015/04/23/why-muslims-are-the-worlds-fastest-growing-religious-group/.

CHAPTER 3
Christianity's Islamic Problem and Solution

Immediately after the creation of humans, God revealed His two primary purposes for humanity (Genesis chapters one and two). This passage reveals that God's will for our lives—yours and mine—is that we know Him and make Him known. God continually affirms these primary purposes throughout the Bible. Throughout the four gospels, Jesus reaffirms this message. After Jesus's death and resurrection, Christians, by and large, sought to fulfill God's primary purposes. They persisted in sharing their faith—and the good news about Christ—for six hundred years. But after the arrival of Islam around AD 600, Christians in MENA typically stopped living out God's main purposes. Specifically, they stopped sharing Christ with Muslims.

Islamic persecution is not what caused Christianity to almost disappear from MENA. Remember, Christians endured persecution for three hundred years after Christ's death and resurrection. Christianity is all but extinct in the MENA region today because of the way Christians *responded* to Islamic persecution. After AD 600 and the birth of Islam, Christians in MENA typically stopped doing the main thing Jesus taught and commanded: sharing the gospel. The Christian response to Islamic persecution was typically the complete opposite to that of earlier Christians who faced persecution from the Roman Empire during the first three hundred years of Christian history. And when they stopped speaking of Christ and seeking to make Him known, the false teaching of Islam took root and spread across the region.

Christians worldwide today are repeating the same costly mistakes Christians in MENA made by not fulfilling the second primary purpose for our lives—to make Him known to everyone, even (or perhaps especially) to Muslims. Unless current trends are reversed, Islam may well become the dominant religion and spread its devastating impact on your area, your country, our world, all of us, and future generations.

Awakening to God's Purposes for Our Lives

After God redeemed me, I was not initially aware that He had already revealed His two primary purposes for our lives. It wasn't until years later, through rereading and restudying the Bible, that I clearly saw God's two main purposes for our lives reaffirmed throughout His word. The Holy Spirit, through that understanding, convicted me of my own failure to fulfill the second aspect of His primary purpose for my life: *to make Him known*. As God opened my eyes to gain more understanding, it became clear that Christianity at large—churches, church leadership, and individual Christians—have also neglected to fulfill this aspect of His purpose.

In addition to revealing God's purpose for humanity, the Bible shows us how missing or neglecting that purpose negatively affects us and our world—and how this has been a problem throughout history; likewise, God's word shows the positive impact we can have by fulfilling His purpose. As we will see in this chapter, this fulfillment or neglect of God's will for us to both know Him *and* make Him known is interconnected to the Islamic problem. As we look at scripture together to better understand God's perspective, we will see how God identifies the problem and offers the solution. God's solution is the only one that has ever worked, and it is the only thing that will turn things around for our world today and for future generations.

God's First Purpose for Your Life

In Genesis 1–2, we are told that God created humankind in His image. It was an act of love: God created us so we can have a personal relationship with Him. A close relationship with God is our primary purpose, and that relationship marks the essence of paradise. God gave us glimpses into paradise in Genesis 1–2 and then again to end the Bible in Revelation 21–22.

God's Second Purpose for Your Life

The second purpose God has for our lives is intertwined with the first. In His first statement to humankind in Genesis 1:28 (ESV), God said, "Be fruitful and multiply and fill the earth. "

God created Adam and Eve so they could have a close relationship with Him, and He told them to fill paradise with human beings so they, too, could have a relationship with Him. Humankind and all other creation on earth initially lived in paradise-like conditions, in perfect harmony and close relationship with God and each other. Throughout the Bible, we see that when paradise is restored, that relationship and harmony will be as well.

God gave us the awesome privilege to fill the earth with bearers of His image. His two primary purposes for your life and mine have not changed; they still are the same since the creation of the first humans.

The Setback

In Genesis 3, Adam and Eve chose to prioritize doing things independently of God and in their own ways instead of His. Humankind has followed suit ever since, choosing to prioritize other gods—most notably and most frequently, the god of self—over the only true God. In short, humankind chose (and continues to choose) to follow Satan's ways and plans instead of God's.

As a result, the relationship between people and God was severed.

Sin radically affected everything, including the harmonious order of creation. Sin replaced paradise-like conditions with evil, suffering, and death. Sin does the same thing today.

But God ...

Sin is a temporary setback, not an end for God's divine program for us. Thank God that as soon as humankind sinned, He immediately implemented His plan of salvation to redeem and restore us into a relationship with Him and a return to paradise through our Lord and Savior Jesus Christ.

Immediately after sin entered the world, God began to reveal His redemption plan in Genesis 3:15. He announced that the woman's child (pointing to Christ) will redeem humanity from Satan and death. The rest of God's unified salvation plan for all of history is revealed through the pages of the Bible; indeed, His plan for salvation is the main plot.

Sin made us lose sight of God's primary purposes for our lives. People continued to be fruitful and multiply, but it was merely in the physical realm. Humanity lost sight of God's desire for people—meaning you and me—to reproduce spiritually, creating image bearers that live eternally in paradise in a close relationship with God.

God reveals a key part of His redemption plan in Genesis 12:2 (ESV) when He tells Abram (later known as Abraham), "And I will make of you a great nation, and I will bless you and make your name great, so that you will be a blessing."

There you have it! A summary from God of what He wants to do with you and me and why He does it.

God set Abraham apart in a unique way to bless him. Since you are reading this book, you are probably already a Christian. That means God in His love set you apart in a unique way to bless you by redeeming you through Jesus as your Lord and Savior.

Genesis 12:2 (ESV) tells us why God blessed Abraham: "So that you will be a blessing."

Do not miss the point here. Just like He did with Abraham, God blessed you with salvation "so that you will be a (salvation) blessing" to others.

As God blesses and saves in the Old Testament, He expects those He saves to: "Tell of his salvation from day to day. Declare his glory among the nations, his marvelous works among all the peoples!" (Psalm 96:2–3 ESV)

God redeemed you to redeem others through you. When you declare His glory among the nations (be that at home or on a far-flung mission field), you are being fruitful and multiplying, and you are fulfilling the second aspect of God's primary purpose for your life. From God's Old Testament perspective, God blessed and saved Christians so that we tell others—including Muslims—about His salvation. Unfortunately, Christians seldom tell Muslims about God's only way of salvation: Jesus Christ as Lord and Savior. The fact that 1.43 billion Muslims, like Sara, have not heard the good news of Jesus as Lord and Savior is evidence of the failure of Christians to fulfill God's purpose for their lives. That is a tremendous problem with terrible implications for Muslims and Christians alike.

The Redeemer Revealed and Reaffirmed

God revealed a key part of His salvation plan in Genesis 12:2 (ESV). The next verse connects His plan to the New Testament: "And in you all the families of the earth shall be blessed."

That blessing was about far more than wealth or property or children; it looks ahead to the ultimate gift: salvation. By sending Jesus, God followed through on His promise to Abraham. It is through Jesus—and only through Jesus—that everyone has access to this blessing of being reconciled to God.

Now let's transition to the New Testament and look at how God describes His two primary purposes for our lives.

In John 15:4 (ESV), Jesus reaffirms and summarizes God's top two primary purposes for you and me:

1. **"Abide in me, and I in you."** God wants us to have an intimate and close relationship with Him. Jesus enables us to have that relationship. We are to abide in Jesus and He in us so we can experience that relationship. Jesus repeats the word *abide* twelve times in John 15:1–17 to reaffirm the importance of a deep relationship with God.
2. **"As the branch cannot bear fruit by itself, unless it abides in the vine, neither can you, unless you abide in me."** In Genesis 1, God commanded humankind to be fruitful and multiply. As noted earlier, being *fruitful* does not simply refer to physical offspring but to spiritual offspring as well. Here in John 15:4, Jesus explains that it is impossible to be fruitful and multiply spiritually unless we abide (have a close and intimate relationship with Him and by extension, God). The words that describe being fruitful and multiplying (bearing fruit) are repeated seven times in John 15:1–17 to reaffirm its importance.

Do not miss this! God wants to have a close relationship with you, and equally important, He wants you to be spiritually fruitful by making Him known to others.

The Mark of a True Child

Loving parents work to have good relationships with their children. They invest time, care, energy, and physical resources into raising their children to be healthy, productive adults. Even as their children mature into adults, parents desire to have a strong, positive relationship with them. Typically, they hope their children will go on to have loving families of their own and produce grandchildren with whom they can enjoy loving, meaningful relationships.

How would you, as a parent, feel if your adult child only contacted you when he or she needed something? What would it feel like to know that the child into whom you invested your love and energy is a lazy, selfish, self-centered adult who wastes all the resources available to him or her on empty and fleeting pleasures?

God, the best and most loving parent ever, seeks a close and intimate relationship with you and me, His beloved children. God invested everything in us so we can be healthy and productive (spiritually fruitful) adults. It honors (glorifies) God when we respond by remaining close with Him (abiding) and by sharing His love with others. Because it is through us that God wants to expand His family and bring more children into His spiritual and eternal kingdom.

In John 15:8 (ESV), Jesus says, "By this my Father is glorified, that you bear much fruit and so prove to be my disciples." Being fruitful is the mark of a true child. Multiplying spiritually is evidence of being a true believer in Jesus, and it is a primary way to glorify God.

God's Purpose for Every Child

God expects us to bear much fruit for the advancement of His kingdom. In other words, He wants us to tell others about Him and His great love for them. After Jesus's resurrection from the dead, and before His ascension back to heaven, Jesus gave His followers a couple of commands that reveal *how* to do that.

One of these commands is found in what is commonly referred to as the Great Commission. In Matthew 28:19 (ESV), Jesus says, "Go therefore and make disciples of all nations. " Luke, the author of Acts, restates this command in Acts 1:8 (ESV). Immediately before Jesus ascended to heaven, He told His followers, "You will be my witnesses ... to the end of the earth."

The words *all nations* and *ends of the earth* make it clear that God intends to offer every people group of every language in the world, without exception, His gift of salvation. That includes Muslims of every language in every Islamic country. But they cannot accept a gift that they know nothing about.

God's Ministry for Every Child

Through Jesus Christ as your Lord and Savior, you have been reconciled to God. In addition to the commands we have from Jesus to "go make disciples of all nations," the apostle Paul explains that each follower of Christ has a ministry from God. Let us review it through several verses in 2 Corinthians 5, beginning with verse 18 (NIV): "All this is from God, who reconciled us to himself through Christ and *gave us the ministry of reconciliation.*"

Yes, you and I have a ministry. In the last section of this book, we will review options for simple, doable actions you can take to help solve our Islamic problem and change the world simply by fulfilling God's purpose for your life. But for now, let's continue with this passage in 2 Corinthians 5: 19–20 (NIV):

> That God was reconciling the world to himself in Christ, not counting people's sins against them. And he has committed to us the message of reconciliation. We are therefore Christ's ambassadors, as though God were making his appeal through us. We implore you on Christ's behalf: Be reconciled to God.

God loves the world and is reconciling the world to Himself. God has given you and me this "message of reconciliation." You are one of God's representatives in the world—an "ambassador" of Christ. God gives you and me the most blessed opportunity (and responsibility) to make His appeal through us to Muslims like Sara.

How did you hear about God's salvation?

How did you first hear about Jesus? Was it from your parents? A friend?

For me, it began with my mom when I was a child, along with other family members, relatives, and friends. And when I walked away from God at age eighteen, I had countless believers in my life who pointed me back to Christ. For twenty years, those ambassadors of God's message of reconciliation patiently reminded me of His love.

That is typically how faith is shared and deepened: Another person (or people), having taken on the role of "ambassador," relates the message of God's reconciliation to you.

The 1.43 billion Muslims in the world today, like Sara, each need a believer to be God's ambassador and share His message of reconciliation with them. They need a Christian to be Jesus's witness with them. They need a Christian like Jane to befriend them and have a relationship with them. They need you and me to be "fruitful and multiply."

Christian Embassy

Changing the world requires at least one Christian embassy (home, small group—not necessarily a church building) in every Islamic area worldwide. Most Islamic areas have none. Locally, in your own city and neighborhood, there are Muslims. These Muslims need a Christian embassy as well.

An embassy represents its nation to the people of the area and proclaims the message given to it by its nation. A Christian embassy represents God to Muslims and proclaims His message of reconciliation that is possible only through Christ. God has already given the message to the embassy, and it is up to believers to open embassies and proclaim His message and to be fruitful and multiply.

There are relatively few Christian embassies actively proclaiming God's message to Muslims. To change the world, we need millions of embassies locally and globally representing God. That means we need tens and hundreds of millions of believers to support and help run effective and functional embassies.

Your Role

With the ministry of reconciliation, God gave each believer the responsibility of supporting the embassy. God gifted you in unique ways and invites you to use your talents to fulfill His purpose for you. Later in the book, we will explore distinct roles in more detail, but for now, I want you to understand that being an ambassador for Christ to Muslims doesn't have to be complicated or difficult. You can, like Jane did with Sara, establish a Christ-centered friendship with a Muslim coworker, neighbor, co-student, etc., and simply love that person as a friend, pray with him or her in the name of Jesus, invite that person to church, and give him or her a Bible as a gift.

A Simple Invitation

Invite a Muslim neighbor, coworker, or international student to dinner around Christmas or Easter. As part of the dinner conversation, ask what he or she thinks Christmas or Easter is about. So many Muslims have misconceptions. Friendly conversations can open the door to sharing what these holidays represent.

Due to their culture of hospitality, the Muslim you invite to dinner is most likely to accept and to invite you to dinner in return. A friendship could be born, like that between Jane and Sara.

If for whatever reason you do not see yourself doing any of the above, perhaps you can be like one of Jane's praying friends who did not interact with Sara directly but encouraged Jane as she befriended Sara and prayed for them both. The point is, you do not necessarily need to be the ambassador who is sharing God's message with a Muslim unless that is your gift and strength. Your role may be one of support, working behind the scenes to encourage and pray for an ambassador who is engaging a Muslim.

A big part of the Islamic problem is that most Christians do not know that we need Christian embassies with Muslims. Most Christians are ignorant of the facts I have shared with you about the spread of Islam. And most Christians are either unaware of God's primary purpose for their lives or have simply neglected to live it out. Now that you are aware of the need and of God's purpose for your life, I hope you will accept God's invitation to be part of the solution by being intentional about becoming spiritually fruitful.

Reflection of the Heart

While it's true that many Christians aren't aware of the need, there are also others who do not care whether we ever have Christian embassies to Muslims. That was my heart prior to 2008, and that attitude is part of our Islamic problem. I used to have a hardened heart toward Muslims. In truth, many Christians (locally and globally) avoid Muslims out of fear, anger, hatred, or indifference.

According to the Bible, however, our purpose as Christians is not dependent upon how we feel toward Muslims (or toward anyone else, for that matter). From God's perspective, as He reveals in the Bible, our response as Christians should be initiated by His love for us. I understand the fears and even the anger some Christians hold toward Muslims, but I also know that the love of Christ compelled me (2 Corinthians 5:14) to become His ambassador. I hope and pray that if you are struggling with a hardened heart, the love of Christ will compel you to become a part of a Christian embassy that is sharing God's message with Muslims and that your heart will be softened when you see the great need.

God's Two Most Important Expectations of You

God saved you, and He expects to use you (as an ambassador in one of His embassies) to save others through you. Throughout the Bible, God drew people to Himself through human relationships. In fact, throughout history and even in your own life, faith is shared most often and most effectively from one person to another.

Whether we become fruitful as God expects us to be reflects our obedience to the two "greatest" commandments God has for each of us.

In Matthew 22:36, religious leaders asked Jesus to identify the "greatest commandment." Jesus responded in two parts. First, He said in Matthew 22:37–38 (NIV), "Love the Lord your God with all your heart and with all your soul and with all your mind. This is the first and greatest commandment."

This commandment can be paraphrased to underscore God's first primary purpose for our lives: be intentional about developing a close and loving relationship with our Creator.

But Jesus did not stop there. In Matthew 22:39 (NIV), He identified the second-greatest commandment: "Love your neighbor as yourself."

This, too, can be paraphrased to point to God's second primary purpose for our lives: Love others enough to point them to God so they can fulfill God's primary purposes for their lives, so we all can be in an eternal relationship together with our Creator.

In the next verse, Jesus drives the point home: "All the law and all the Prophets hang on these two commandments."

I shared with you that God had to transform my heart toward Muslims. Before 2008, I did not fully understand or appreciate the meaning of Matthew 22:36–40 (NIV). If you do not already fully understand these verses, please stop right now and pray that the Holy Spirit will reveal the truth to you of what I am going to share with you in the rest of this book.

Within the broader context of what God reveals in the above verses is that if we genuinely love God, then we will also love our neighbors. The two greatest commandments go together, and *all* of God's revealed word to us is summed up in these two commandments. When God's love is truly in our hearts, we are compelled to love our neighbors. The depth of our love for God is revealed and reflected in our loving actions to others.

Our Muslim neighbors, those who live next door and those who live on the other side of the world—all 1.43 billion of them—need to know the good news about Jesus. The willingness of Christians to become part of an embassy and/or act as ambassadors of Christ is a revelation and reflection of their love toward God. Remember that we prove ourselves as followers of Jesus when we abide in Him and bear spiritual fruit.

I pray that the Holy Spirit helps you feel the weight of Jesus's words in your heart, soul, and mind.

> For this is the love of God, that we keep his commandments. And his commandments are not burdensome. (1 John 5:3 ESV)

The First and Foundational Essential for Every Christian to Know and Do

In summary of the previous two chapters, the first of the five essentials for every Christian to know and do is share the good news of Jesus Christ as Lord and Savior with a lost world—including Muslims.

All five essentials are interconnected, like grooves of a key that unlocks the heart of a Muslim for the gospel, resulting in multiplying fruit. I will reveal the other four essentials later in the book. I will share stories to teach how they work together and how you can do them and be involved so together we can significantly increase numbers to grow the minority to become the most effective majority—to help change the world.

The earlier two chapters revealed how simple it all can be as modeled by Jane. She befriended and cared for a Muslim, she shared the gospel with her by bringing her to church and giving her a Bible, and she prayed with her in the name of Jesus. Jane's simple actions were a spark that began a chain reaction of multiplication, resulting so far with thousands of Muslims hearing the gospel for the first time, with hundreds already accepting Jesus as Lord and Savior.

Your simple actions could be another spark for another multiplying movement.

CHAPTER 4
Ramifications of our Response

Sherry was born and raised in a Muslim family in an Islamic nation. She was a devout Muslim girl, very knowledgeable in the Quran and the Islamic religion. Although she had met some Christians growing up, they never shared with her the good news of salvation through Jesus as Lord and Savior.

Looking for more educational opportunities and a better life, Sherry moved to a Western nation as an international student. Like most Muslims, Sherry believed Western nations were Christian nations and therefore, that every person from that nation must be a Christian—including the students of the college she attended.

Sherry was horrified to see these "Christian" students doing what she learned in Islam as extremely immoral behavior: partaking in drugs, alcohol, and illicit sexual relations. Sherry's parents and siblings in North Africa were also horrified by the stories she told them about her classmates. They urged Sherry to connect with the Islamic community in the area that would help prevent her from being corrupted by the immoral behavior of "Christian" students.

Obediently, Sherry found a mosque close to her and became more devout than ever before. She even took a class on how to effectively share her Muslim faith with Christians, with the goal of converting some to Islam.

Sherry soon discovered that it was exceedingly difficult to find a Christian who would engage her in spiritual conversations. And when she did find Christians who were willing to talk, they did not seem to know much about either religion and weren't able to hold a meaningful discussion about their holy book, the Bible, much less the Quran.

Finally, she found one student, Samantha, who would gladly talk to her. Like the other Christians Sherry had met, Samantha was not able to "debate" any of the issues or adequately answer Sherry's challenging questions about Christianity, but she was happy to give Sherry her Bible. Frustrated, Sherry decided she needed to read the Bible herself to discover what the Christian students were supposed to believe. She thought that perhaps if she began there, she might discover the path to lead them into Islam.

Once Sherry began studying the Bible on her own, she could not stop reading it. No longer was she reading the Bible with the goal of converting Christians to Islam but to quench her own insatiable thirst for the truth. As she compared the teachings of the Quran and the Bible, Sherry grew to love Jesus and came to believe that the Bible is the true word of God. Six months after she started studying the Bible, Sherry accepted Jesus as Lord and Savior.

iHOPE was created to be an embassy. Part of our mission is to be a place where Muslims like Sherry can connect to ask questions about Christianity and the Bible. Another part of our mission is to help prepare Christians to be effective in their roles as part of the solution. To do that, we offer equipping classes for Christians who want to take Jesus's message to the nations and specifically to Muslims. During these classes, we take groups to tour mosques (Muslim places of worship, like churches are for Christians) in various cities in Christianized nations. While there, we respectfully observe a Muslim prayer and worship service and talk with a few people in attendance. The followings stories occurred on the same visit to a mosque in Texas and are typical of the mosque tours we conduct.

Christian Mother Converts to Islam

Our friendly Muslim host, Mary, was an American mother of three young children. Mary took us to an observation room next to the main worship center of the mosque. A glass wall separated the observation room from the worship room so our class could see and hear the prayer/worship service without being a distraction.

Before the service began, Mary shared her testimony with us, explaining why she converted to Islam. Mary's father is a pastor of a church, and she grew up in a Christian home. But Mary was disillusioned by the hypocrisy she says she saw in the lives of the Christians she knew. While in college, a Muslim befriended Mary and shared the Islamic faith with her. That began a Quran study journey for Mary and eventual conversion from Christianity to Islam.

As part of her discipleship in learning to be a good Muslim, Mary told us she had attended Islamic evangelism classes. In these classes (which are ongoing), Muslims are taught how to effectively share their faith with the people of their new country, especially with Christians. Men are taught how to share their faith with other men, women with women, and even children with children. Muslims are highly encouraged to invite Christians to mosque services and special evangelistic events in mosques that are tailored to Christians.

One of our students asked Mary if Christians typically shared their faith with Muslims who come to that mosque and if some Muslims there converted to Christianity as a result. Mary said that it is rare for Christians to share their faith with Muslims. And if they do, the mosque does an excellent job of preparing their Muslim congregation to remain in their Islamic faith.

Christian Student Converts to Islam

Four hundred or so Muslims packed into the mosque that night for prayer and worship. Before the worshipers were dismissed, the *imam* (a Muslim cleric) invited a young man called Mark to the front of the room. Mark introduced himself as a twenty-year-old American college student. He had decided to convert to Islam.

In his brief testimony, Mark shared that a Muslim international student had befriended him in college, invited him to mosque prayers, and studied the Quran with him. Mark grew up in a Christian home, but he was drawn by his Muslim's friends' zeal for the Islamic religion. Mark said he did not see the same passion or commitment to Christianity from his Christian family or friends. Mark said Muslims were much more committed to Allah than Christians were to God.

Mark then said the Islamic Shahada in front of everyone. Shahada is the Muslim profession of faith. Translated to English, the Shahada states: "There is no god but Allah, and Muhammad is the messenger of Allah." The Shahada to a Muslim is like a baptism is to a new Christian. By saying the Shahada, Mark was agreeing to the full religion of Islam and all its beliefs.

Muslims' Outreach toward Christians

Throughout my life in MENA and in the United Sates, I observed that Muslims are significantly more evangelistic with Christians than Christians are toward Muslims. That means they are more obedient to what they believe God is calling them to do, which is to spread Islam worldwide. They intentionally and strategically target Christians because they see Christianity as the only other evangelical religion in the world.

In contrast, the majority of Christians have not shared the good news about Jesus as their Lord and Savior with Muslims. This reality has tremendous and lasting implications for you, me, our children, and future generations and has resulted in one of the most urgent and important problems of our times.

What Happens When Muslims Evangelize and Christians Don't?

Because most Christians are not evangelistic toward Muslims, and Muslims tend to be very evangelistic toward Christians, Islam is growing. This disparity is the reason once-Christianized areas, like where I grew up in MENA, are now up to 99 percent Muslim. It is also the reason Islam is on the rise in the United Kingdom, the United States, and in other nations worldwide. If current trends continue, it is not a matter of if but rather *when* Islam will become the majority religion in many currently Christianized nations.

Islam in the United States

Approximately 3.3 million Muslims live in America today, and that number is expected to grow to 8.1 million by 2050.[15] A 2005 article from *The New York Times* notes that an estimated 25 percent of the Muslims in the United States—approximately 825,000 people—converted to Islam while living in America.[16]

Think about that: around 825,000 men and women in America, like Mark and Mary, converted to Islam—many of them from Christianity.

To put that number in perspective, as of January 2015, there were 564,708 homeless people in the United States.[17] The number of converts to Islam in America is larger than the nation's homeless population. In every major city, and even in small towns, we can see

---

[15] "A new estimate of the U.S. Muslim population," *Pew Research Center,* Jan. 6, 2016, http://www.pewresearch.org/fact-tank/2016/01/06/a-new-estimate-of-the-u-s-muslim-population/.

[16] Andrea Elliot, "Muslim converts face discrimination," *The New York Times,* Apr. 30, 2005, https://www.nytimes.com/2005/04/30/nyregion/muslim-converts-face-discrimination.html?_r=0.

[17] "Homelessness in America," *National Alliance to End Homelessness,* Accessed Oct. 12, 2018, http://www.endhomelessness.org/pages/snapshot_of_homelessness.

the plight of the homeless. Many churches have outreach or ministries dedicated to helping these people find food, shelter, work, medical attention, and most importantly, hope in Christ. But how many of these same churches have programs to reach out to Muslims? As we consider the Islamic problem, we must recognize that, although our Muslim neighbors may have shelter and plenty of food, they do not have the one thing they really need: Jesus.

Mosques in America

When Sara (the former Muslim whose story I shared in chapter 2) first moved to the United States, the metropolitan area in her midwestern state had only one mosque with a congregation of about three hundred Muslims. Twenty years later, this same area is home to seventy-four mosques and about two hundred fifty thousand Muslims.

When I moved to the Dallas/Fort Worth area of Texas in 2010, I looked into how many mosques were within a thirty-mile radius from me. I found seventeen. When I moved out of the area in June 2015, there were seventy-two mosques within that same radius.

The first "purpose-built" mosque in America was built around 1921. In 1970, there were 100 mosques in the United States. Over the next thirty years that number continued to grow, and by the year 2000, there were 1,209 mosques in the United States. In only ten years, that number had almost doubled to 2,106 in 2010.[18] As of 2015, the number of mosques in the United States was 2,582.[19]

---

[18] 17 "Islamic places of worship in U.S. up 74% since 2000," USATODAY.com, Accessed 2018-12-21,
http://usatoday30.usatoday.com/news/religion/story/2012-02-29/islamic-worship-growth-us/53298792/1.

[19] "The most comprehensive guide to mosques and Islamic schools," *salatomatic,* Accessed Oct. 12, 2018, http://www.salatomatic.com/reg/United-States/sPpaNwWSpq.

Islam in Europe and Asia

Islam is the fastest-growing religion in Europe. The Muslim population grew from 19.5 million in 2010 to 25.8 million in 2016 and is expected to hit 58 million by 2050. (These numbers exclude Turkey, which is 98 percent Muslim.)

In Asia and the Asia-Pacific region, Islam is the most prevalent religion. In 1990, 21.6 percent of that region was Muslim. By 2010, that percentage had grown to 24.8 percent of the population. It is estimated that by 2030, Muslims will grow to become 27.3 percent of the population.[20]

Islam on the Rise Worldwide

Islam is the fastest-growing religion in the world, expanding at more than twice the rate of Christianity. Statistics gathered by the Pew Research Center indicate that, at the current rates, Islam will be close to catching up with Christianity as the world's leading religion by 2050.

Numerically, Christianity will continue to grow. In 2010, there were 2.17 billion Christians worldwide. At the current rates, Christianity is expected to grow to 2.92 billion worldwide by 2050. But as a percentage of the world's population, Christianity is expected to remain stagnant. In 2010, Christianity represented 31.4 percent of the world's population, and it is projected to be the same in 2050.

Islam, meanwhile, is growing both numerically and as a percentage of the world's population. In 2010, there were 1.6 billion Muslims worldwide, and that number is projected to grow to 2.76 billion in 2050. In 2010, Muslims were 23.2 percent of the world's population, but in 2050 they are projected to grow to 29.7 percent. Then by 2070,

---

[20] *"The Future of the Global Muslim Population (Asia)."* Pew Research Center. 27 January 2011. Retrieved 27 December 2017.

Islam is projected to overtake Christianity as the largest religious group in the world.[21]

What all these numbers mean is that, wherever you live, Islam is probably growing there. The question is, *how do we turn these trends around*?

A Matter of Wise Perspective

It is time to accept the reality that Muslims are moving into Christian (and post-Christian) countries, and they will continue to do so. The Muslim population in Western countries will continue to grow through both high birth rates as well as aggressive evangelism and converts unless Christians step up and accept their role—our role—as part of the solution to Islamic problem.

The influx of Muslims to Christianized nations worldwide in recent years presents the greatest gospel *opportunity* we have ever had with Muslims. I am not alone in the belief that it is precisely because Christians have not persistently taken the message of Christ to Muslim nations that we now have this opportunity in our own hometowns. God will make sure His will is done, which in this case seems to mean that because Christians have been largely unwilling to go in adequate numbers to reach Muslims, God is bringing them to us.

Unfortunately, many Christians believe that Muslims and Islam are the greatest threat to Christianity and to a free society and way of life.[22] While it's true that *Islam* poses an extreme threat to Christianity and to personal freedom, we shouldn't view our Muslim neighbors as such. Rather, it is my hope and prayer that every Christian and church will view Muslims as people in need of God's love and salvation.

---

[21] "The Future of World Religions: Population Growth Projections, 2015–2050," *Pew Research Center,* Apr. 2, 2015, http://www.pewforum.org/2015/04/02/religious-projections-2010-2050/.

[22] "Tensions with Secularism and Modernity," Pew Research Center, June 22, 2011, http://www.pewforum.org/2011/06/22/global-survey-tensions/.

History *with* the Gospel

By now I hope it is abundantly clear that the primary biblical key to changing the world is to spread the good news of Jesus as Lord and Savior. History has proven that obedience to what Jesus commands is the best way to protect Christianity, our nations, our families, and our future. Before we move on, I want us to look back at how God's mission has unfolded since the birth of Christ. I believe it is essential to study and remember what has happened in the past—and be aware of what is happening in the present—to understand why and how these things shape the world. Let's review a few lessons relevant to you and me today from a summary of first-century biblical history and how it has impacted our world today and will impact the future.

Biblical Warnings

The history in the Bible reveals the devastating impact on the world when humankind does not fulfill God's primary purposes. Let's briefly review the impact of the cycle of failure on display throughout the Bible but specifically in regard to humankind not fulfilling God's second primary purpose, to be fruitful and multiply.

The cycle of failure began with Adam and Eve. Within a generation, they went from walking with God daily in paradise to where they had only one godly son who was murdered by his own brother (Genesis 4). Within one generation, their own children stopped fulfilling God's primary purposes for their lives. That resulted in the flood of Genesis 6–7. Noah's family was redeemed from the flood, and they saw God's awesome power and holiness on display; still, within a generation, they stopped fulfilling God's primary purposes for their lives.

That cycle continues throughout the Old Testament of the Bible. Abraham is saved, and then within a few generations, his descendants stop fulfilling God's primary purposes for their lives.

God then redeems Israel as a nation so they can be a model for the rest of the world that had already walked away from God. But we see this human cycle of failure on display throughout their history. Typically, within a generation, they failed to fulfill God's second primary purpose for them regardless of the awesome things they had seen God do.

As a result, Israel went from being God's special nation on earth to almost disappearing entirely by the time Jesus came to earth around two thousand years ago.

Government-Ordered Massacre

When Jesus was born, the Romans were the godless conquerors and brutal rulers of His people, the Jewish nation. Jesus came to save the world, but Satan tried to kill Him off first through Herod the Great. King Herod ruled Judea under the Roman Empire from around 37 to 4 BC. In an attempt to kill Jesus as a baby, Herod ordered troops to kill all the male children in Bethlehem who were two years old or younger (Matthew 2:16).

Herod Antipas succeeded his father as king from 4 BC to AD 39. John the Baptist and Jesus were killed under the rule of Herod Antipas. Jesus knew the whole story before it happened; He knew of the deadly persecutions Herod (father and then son) would inflict on Him and His followers. Yet Jesus taught His followers to respond to the Roman Empire's tyranny by sharing the gospel. We are to continue to be witnesses for Jesus, the only Savior, with the only message that can save a dying world.

Persecution and Opposition

When Jesus sent out His followers to tell people about Him and His Father, He warned them that they would face persecution—even death. He also encouraged them and equipped them to respond to opposition and persecution. The following is a summary of some of the teachings of Jesus found in Matthew 10, as well as 16:24–28 and 25:14–30:

1. Proclaim the good news to all.
2. In the process, we will face persecution.
3. We may even lose our temporary, earthly life.
4. Even so, persist. Do not fear those who oppose, persecute, or even kill.
5. God's reward for us is infinitely greater than anything we may lose, and it will last for eternity.

The Result of Obedience

After Jesus ascended to heaven, His followers became more emboldened and persistent in their efforts to tell others about Jesus. The persecution they endured was equally persistent. When Stephen became the first Christian martyr (Acts 7:54–60), his death ushered in even greater levels of persecution of Christians, which intensified further under Roman Emperor Nero (AD 54–68). Nero slaughtered Christians in horrific ways, and that began government-sanctioned massacres of Christians. This continued with Domitian between AD 81–96.

The last book of the Bible, Revelation, is believed to have been written during and/or between the reigns of Nero and Domitian, sometime between AD 54 and 96. Regardless of the exact year, we know that the apostle John wrote Revelation during a time of horrific massacres of Christians. With that in mind, Revelation 6:9 (NLT) states: "I saw under the altar the souls of all who had been martyred for the word of God and for being faithful in their testimony."

These first-century Christians faithfully shared the good news. They responded to persecutions, even unto horrible deaths, in obedience to God. In Revelation 6:10 the persecuted souls asked the Lord how much longer the suffering would endure. Notice God's answer in 6:11 (NLT): "And they were told to rest a little longer until the full number of their brothers and sisters, their fellow servants of Jesus who were to be martyred, had joined them."

In Revelation God teaches perseverance for the faithful Christians because war against them due to their testimony of Jesus will continue till Christ returns. In Revelation 13:10 (NLT), God puts it this way: "Anyone who is destined for prison will be taken to prison. Anyone destined to die by the sword will die by the sword. This means God's holy people must endure persecution patiently and remain faithful."

The Christians of the first few centuries kept sharing the good news of Jesus. They also kept getting persecuted, even unto death, culminating in the great persecutions under Roman Emperors Diocletian and Galerius (AD 284–311). Three centuries of persecution finally ended in 313 when Constantine legalized Christianity in the Roman Empire.

How did Christians, who began with a small group of people led by twelve disciples, transform the mighty Roman Empire? Revelation 12:11 (NLT) reveals the answer: "By the blood of the Lamb and by their testimony. And they did not love their lives so much that they were afraid to die."

With daring faith, they shared the good news about Jesus with their persecutors and their enemies. Armed with only the gospel, this small group of ordinary folks (most were uneducated and had low-paying occupations, such as fishermen) transformed the Roman Empire. It was costly. With the exception of John, who was persecuted and exiled, it is believed the rest of the disciples were all martyred in some horrible way.

Impact of Early Christians on You

Despite extreme persecution, this small but obedient group accomplished much. By AD 600, much of the known world was Christianized, including the Middle East, North Africa, and southern Europe. From there, Christianity spread throughout the world to your nation and now your family. Without the faithful obedience of early Christians to share the gospel, you might have never learned about God's love for you.

The Result of Disobedience

As I mentioned in chapter 1, things changed after AD 600. Specifically, the typical Christian response to persecution changed from one of persistence to that of anger, hate, indifference, and fear. Wherever Islam took root, Christians stopped sharing the good news about Jesus, thus disobeying God's commandments to do so.

Without the gospel, the Middle East and North Africa (MENA) is now up to 99 percent Muslim. And without the gospel, Islam is growing at twice the rate of Christianity[23] and forecast to surpass it as the largest religion in the world by 2070.[24]

Even in most Christianized nations, Muslims are not befriended by Christians;[25] no one shares the gospel with them. As a result, what happened in MENA to turn a Christianized area into up to 99 percent Muslim is now happening slowly but surely in Christianized nations in your area.

History Is Repeating Itself

This biblical history repeated itself in MENA and is now repeating itself elsewhere, as is evident in the recent decline of Christianity in historically Christianized nations. For example, in the United States in 1956, 96 percent of Americans identified themselves as Christian,

---

[23] Michael Lipka and Conrad Hacket, "Why Muslims are the world's fastest-growing religious group," *Pew Research Center,* April 6, 2017, http://www.pewresearch.org/fact-tank/2015/04/23/why-muslims-are-the-worlds-fastest-growing-religious-group/.

[24] "The Future of World Religions: Population Growth Projections, 2015–2050," *Pew Research Center,* Apr. 2, 2015, http://www.pewforum.org/2015/04/02/religious-projections-2010-2050/.

[25] Natalie Crowson, "Perfect Strangers: Christians Living Among Buddhists, Hindus and Muslims," *Lausanne Movement,* 2007, http://www.lausanneworldpulse.com/research.php/856.

with 1 percent as non-religious.[26] Then a slow but steady decline of Christianity began, and in 2015, 70 percent of Americans identified themselves as Christian; meanwhile, the non-religious category grew steadily to 17 percent by 2015. Current projections reveal an ongoing decrease for Christianity as a percentage of the population in America. By 2050, unless things change, 65.8 percent of Americans will identify themselves as Christian, and the non-religious category is expected to increase to around 25 percent.[27]

In Europe, 74.5 percent of the population in 2010 identified themselves as Christian. But that is expected to continue declining slowly but steadily to 65.2 percent of the population by 2050.[28]

It's Time to Turn Things Around

The best way to turn the trends around is the best solution Jesus gave and commanded: share the good news of Jesus Christ as Lord and Savior with Muslims.

I personally met hundreds of Muslims who worship at the mosque Sherry attended before she became a Christian. Most of them do not initiate contact with a Christian, but they pray for and encourage Muslims like Sherry who do. They also financially support the evangelical efforts of the mosque and of Muslims like Sherry, including making sure she has all the material and tools she needs to be successful.

- What if churches like yours decided to become intentionally evangelistic with Muslims in your area, like how your local mosque is most likely evangelistic with the Christians there?

---

[26] "Religion," *Gallup,* Accessed Oct. 12, 2018, http://www.gallup.com/poll/1690/religion.aspx.http://www.gallup.com/poll/1690/religion.aspx.

[27] "Christians," *Pew Research Center,* Apr. 2, 2015, http://www.pewforum.org/2015/04/02/christians/.http://www.pewforum.org/2015/04/02/christians/

[28] Ibid.

- What if churches like yours decided to equip Christians to share their faith with Muslims intentionally and effectively, like Sherry's mosque did with her?
- What if Christians like you decided to get equipped and intentionally seek Muslims in your area to build gospel-centered relationships with them?

I have seen this happen in a few churches, and perhaps you and your church are already doing so. Wherever churches or individual Christians do the biblical principles that Jesus taught, Muslims are coming to faith in Christ, and there is a harvest. But we need churches and Christians in every area to do so.

Don't Get Distracted from *Your* Purpose

God has two main purposes for humans' lives. Even as we try to live out God's purpose, a spiritual battle wages all around us. Satan and his army are constantly fighting in hopes to achieve their own mission. In summary, Satan wants to lead the whole world astray (Revelation 12:9) from God.

Satan's mission is to prevent us from fulfilling God's two primary purposes for our lives. If you are a Christian, Satan and his demons have already failed in their first objective. When you became a believer, God—through Jesus—restored you into a relationship with Him.

But Satan is persistent. He knows he can't take you from God's grasp (John 10:28), so he and his demons are constantly fighting to distract you from your mission to glorify God by telling others about Him. This spiritual battle was raging when Adam and Eve were created. Satan even tried to defeat Jesus by trying to distract Him from His purpose while He was on earth. (See Matthew 4:1–11.) Thank God that Jesus remained focused and defeated Satan by fulfilling His purpose of saving the world! The point is, this spiritual battle is constant, and it will continue until the second coming of Christ when He banishes Satan and his demons. You and I must be diligent. We cannot afford to allow Satan to distract us from God's primary purposes for our lives. We must not become so busy or hard-hearted that we forget our most important mission.

Throughout His ministry, Jesus taught His followers the response to persecution and opposition was to persist in sharing the gospel. This remains our only viable response to Islam today. Pointing others toward Christ is the way you and I can help transform the world. It means befriending Muslims, like Jane did with Sara, or simply giving a Muslim a Bible, like Mary did with Sherry. It means praying for and equipping Christians who go to the places where sharing the gospel is illegal and talk with people one on one. It may even mean going to those places yourself.

CHAPTER 5
Solution in Your Area

Many of the Christians who have met Sara from chapter 2 or heard her story tell me that they do not have a problem with Muslims like Sara. Their concerns are with the 10 percent of Muslims who have the propensity to be radicalized. Those concerns aren't unfounded.

With 1.68 billion Muslims worldwide, 10 percent equates to around 168 million Muslims. That is a lot of radicals, and any one of them could become a terrorist. And that's the fear that Christians (and non-Christians, for that matter) have regarding Islamic radicals: the harm and terror they want to inflict on the world in the name of Allah. Some Christians fear that these radicals are attempting to infiltrate our neighborhoods, take over our country, and institute Islamic sharia law, etc. (They are, and they do.) They watch and wonder about what to do to ensure the ongoing conflicts associated with Islam do not come to their nations, cities, and neighborhoods.

Perhaps you share those concerns. You, too, may wonder, "What do we do with Muslims who are trying to come to my area? What do we do legally, militarily, or politically? What do we do with Islamic radicals who are already here?"

If so, you aren't alone. The following story offers insight into these kinds of questions and concerns. You'll also see how world changers are responding to possible Islamic radicals who may have infiltrated our neighborhoods.

A Muslim Jihadist Moves Next Door

Sam was born into a large Muslim family in an Islamic nation. Recruited as a child by an extremist Islamic organization, Sam became convinced in the righteousness of their views toward infidels.

Instead of seeking martyrdom for Allah and Islam, Sam's strategy was to become a stealth cultural jihadist. He intended to move to the United States to lead a movement to convert Christians to Islam. Sam was to help conquer the Western world, one Christian at a time. Although immigration security screening is designed to identify Islamic extremists and deny them an entry visa, Sam somehow successfully passed the process and legally entered the United States.

Sam's ultimate goal was to help make America a Muslim nation under Islamic Sharia law. He thought it best to strike in a place where Christians seemed the most dedicated to their religion. So, at twenty years old, Sam moved to the Bible Belt, where he worked for years as a stealth jihadist to convert Christians to Islam.

World Changers to the Rescue

Sam's work came to an abrupt halt when he was seriously injured in a car accident. He initially thought Allah had brought his jihad to a premature end. Sitting in the wreckage and unable to move, he felt certain he was going to die. Finally, Christian men who were passing by pulled over and called for an ambulance. That call helped save Sam's life.

Of course, the men did not know of Sam's Islamic views. But Sam knew these men were Christians. Their loving act to a stranger was the first seed of Christlike love ever planted in Sam's heart.

At the hospital, Sam learned that his neck was broken in two places. Surgeries to repair the damage were successful, but the hospital could not discharge him without someone to take responsibility to care for him in a home. Sam had no one in America. Joe, one of Sam's doctors, was a Christian. Joe knew Sam was a Muslim from the Middle East.

Joe also knew Sam was all alone in a foreign land, and that he needed a place where he could get help to recover. Joe responded to God's love and invited Sam to be his guest until he was fully recovered.

Sam accepted the invitation of Joe, the infidel. To his surprise, Joe and his Christian family welcomed him, a Muslim stranger, into their home and treated him like a dearly beloved member of the family. Christian friends of Joe's family also rallied to help Sam recover physically.

When they learned that Sam was unable to pay the huge medical bills brought on by the accident, Joe's family and friends invited other believers to meet Sam and help with his financial needs. They ended up raising the money to cover Sam's bills and had enough left over to buy Sam a car. Sam was overwhelmed by the outpouring of unconditional Christian love and generosity toward him.

All these believers simply loved on Sam the Muslim. They cleaned him when he was unable to clean himself, fed him when he could not feed himself, and covered for him financially when he had no money. They prayed for him in the name of Jesus and spoke openly about the faith that underscored everything they did.

Changing a Jihadist's Heart

Before the accident, Sam thought Christians were evildoers. He'd come to the United States as a stealth cultural jihadist on a mission to convert Christians to Islam.

After the accident, believers befriended Sam. While at Joe's home, and for the first time in his life, Sam experienced Christlike love, received prayers in the name of Jesus, and heard the good news about Christ as Lord and Savior. These things were the catalysts that softened Sam's hard heart and shattered his Islamic radical worldview.

After Sam was healthy enough to take care of himself, Joe's family sent him home with a gift: a Bible. In the privacy of his home, Sam began to pray, begging God to reveal the truth to him. As Sam read the Bible, God did reveal the truth, and Sam became a believer in Jesus Christ as his Lord and Savior.

Christian Embassy to an Islamic Jihadist

Joe and his Christian friends were Jesus's witnesses to Sam the Islamic jihadist in their neighborhood. They were ambassadors for God in the ministry of reconciliation. As a result, God used them to transform Sam to a world changer. Today Sam is doing with Muslims what Joe and the other believers did with him. Sam is being fruitful and multiplying, helping change the world, one heart at a time.

What would you do with a Muslim jihadist neighbor?

Role of the Government

A small percentage of Muslims, perhaps 10 percent, are extremists like Sam was. Yet that small percentage could add up to around 168 million Islamic extremists around the world. Many Islamic extremists would love to become established in a Western nation.

What should we do about that?

What *can* we do about that?

Christians often ask me questions like these, and I always refer people to the Bible for answers. The Bible offers principles that make it clear that the government, church, and the citizens have distinct roles to fill.

Regarding the threats from Islamic radicals and terrorists, state and federal lawmakers in every nation work to balance security and immigration laws. The hope is that they can implement laws and screening processes that prevent Islamic extremists from entering their countries in the first place. If God gifted you as a politician, diplomat, or lawmaker, please be part of the solution. And if you are involved in security, the military, or law enforcement, I am grateful for you for risking your life to protect others.

Role of the Citizen

Most Christians, however, are not serving in a government-related role, so what do they do regarding this subject?

The entire Bible makes it clear that you ought to be a good citizen (two examples are Romans 13:1 and Titus 3:1–2) of the nation where you live. One example of how you can do that is through voting. Whenever you can vote, please make wise choices and vote in elections for government leaders who will serve God as they do their job as leaders.

The other thing the Bible teaches is that we are to pray for our leaders in government. Three examples of that are Jeremiah 29:7, 1 Timothy 2:1–4, and 1 Peter 2:13–14, 17. Pray that God will give the people in government and security wisdom and discernment. Pray for their protection as they help protect us.

Also, if you have reason to suspect someone is a terrorist, report that person to the appropriate authority so the professionals can assess the situation and deal with a potential threat.

Role of the Christian

Regardless of what any government or professional agency does or does not do, your role as a Christian remains the same. The Bible is very clear that, regardless of your job or position in life, God gives you the most blessed opportunity to be involved as part of a Christian embassy. No matter why a Muslim ends up in your neighborhood, God expects you to serve as He gifted you, wholeheartedly, as Jesus's witnesses in God's ministry of reconciliation.

It is easy to be distracted by news media and the day-to-day struggles of life, and in the process, lose sight of God's primary purpose for our lives. Joe and his friends remained faithful to God, and their obedience helped Sam find his Savior.

What Good Can Come from Having an Islamic Jihadist Neighbor?

Know this: If a Muslim jihadist like Sam slips through government screenings and ends up in your area of the world, it is not an accident. The Bible is clear that God is in complete control. If a Muslim (jihadist or not) becomes your neighbor, then God allowed it. Muslims are coming to Western nations because God is allowing it.

Why would God allow undercover Islamic terrorists, Islamic extremists, or stealth jihadists into your area?

Philippians 1:12 (Berean Study Bible) summarizes a biblical answer to questions like that: "Now I want you to know, brothers, that my circumstances have actually served to advance the gospel."

That means that if any Muslim is in your area, God is intentionally giving you a most blessed gospel opportunity to be fruitful and multiply. I encourage you to explore opportunities to build gospel-centered relationships with Muslims. A gospel-centered relationship is one where you are looking for practical opportunities to share the good news about Jesus as Lord and Savior.

Joe and his Christian family and friends did exactly that with Sam. They had no idea of Sam's intentions as a stealth jihadist. The fact is, his intentions didn't matter. Demonstrating God's love and sharing the gospel were what was most important, and those were the only things that could have ever changed Sam's heart.

Understanding the Needs of Muslims in Your Area Is Key

Regardless of why a Muslim comes to your area or whether they are more like Sam (a stealth jihadist) or Sara (an immigrant with no ill intent, simply seeking a better life), they typically experience a similar set of emotions in the first couple of years in a Western country: culture shock, sadness, loneliness, emptiness, regret, and hopelessness. These emotions almost always lead to some level of depression.

Without Christian friends stepping in to help fill that void, a

Muslim typically ends up surrounding him or herself with other Muslims. Many become more devout than they were in the country they came from, like Sara and Sherry did. Because they are not befriended by someone in their neighborhood, they feel undesirable, and some Muslims further isolate themselves. The sense of rejection may make them feel bitter or angry towards their neighbors, which in turn can make them vulnerable to extremist views and more susceptible to radicalization.

Having at least one Christian friend can fill one of the most basic needs a Muslim immigrant has. Befriending a Muslim in your area is a biblical way to meet that need. In my experience, gospel-centered friendships also appear to help prevent radicalization. In Sam's case, it transformed an existing jihadist.

The world needs more believers like Jane and Joe, who view their Muslim neighbors as divine appointments by God. The increasing number of Muslims to Christianized nations—to your area—represents unprecedented gospel opportunities. Within the gospel is God's power to transform lives. I hope you will accept these divine appointments, step out in obedient faith, and help change the world one heart at a time, beginning in your area.

The Butterfly Effect and You

The butterfly effect is the scientific idea that the smallest action, like the flap of a butterfly wing, can, through time, effect change in major ways worldwide.

Imagine how exciting it was for Jane and Joe to witness how their simple, obedient actions contributed to Sara's and Sam's salvation and transformation. Now Jane and Joe witness the gospel at work in Sara and Sam as they share the hope of Jesus with Muslims, both locally and globally.

Do you dare believe that God called you, equipped you with the Holy Spirit, and could work mightily in and through you?

Have you made the connection between the time and place in which you live and God's call upon you?

The events concerning Muslims today are not catching God by surprise. God placed you precisely where you are and put this book in your hand for a purpose. History is filled with examples of Christians who believed that God would work through them to make a significant difference for His kingdom. Will you allow God to use you to make a difference for this and future generations?

CHAPTER 6
A "Glocal" Solution

Some Christians tell me they are happy to share the good news of Jesus with the Muslims God sends to their country. But with constant news reports of extremist acts and millions of people seeking refuge from Islamic-related terror, they feel powerless to make any real difference on a larger scale. Maybe you can relate to that sense of frustration.

The two stories I'll share with you in this chapter will help you see how your biblical response to Muslims in your neighborhood or city *can* make a powerful difference in the lives of people worldwide. You'll learn how one Christian sharing the good news about Jesus with a Muslim can impact countless Muslims globally, including those in places like Iran or who are involved in conflicts such as the Arab/Israeli one. In other words, your actions locally have a global effect, which is where we get the word *glocal*. And in our very connected modern world, it can be remarkably simple to be fruitful and multiply *glocally* by sharing the good news of Christ.

A Window into Iran

Amal and her husband, Ali, were born and raised in Iran. Iran is considered an Islamic extremist country by many of the world's other countries. Ali and Amal were devout Muslims; however, they were nonextremists. They raised their children to be nonextremists as well. Ali is a surgeon, and Amal is a medical doctor. They were wealthy both financially and in terms of having a large, close extended family.

Authoritarian religious rulers govern Iran. It has a contentious history with Western nations, many of which consider the country to be an "enemy" or "terrorist" state. Like many Muslim Iranians, Ali and Amal held a negative view of Western nations. They believed Western Christians were immoral in comparison to Muslims and were anti-Muslim and anti-Iran.

At the same time, Ali and Amal believed the quality of non-religious education was better in certain institutions in Western nations. They desired the best-quality educational opportunities for their children and decided to move temporarily to a Western nation so their children could complete their education.

Given their beliefs about Western nations, Amal and Ali were genuinely concerned about moving away from their spiritually moral country, culture, and extended family and friends—and into a strange and immoral society. They believed, however, that they and their children were very solid Muslims, which would help them remain faithful to their religion and good morals.

Before they selected the location of their temporary country of residence, they searched for good educational institutions that were close to other Iranian Muslims. They found good schools close to a mosque with a good reputation. They moved to a Western nation and immediately began to make new Muslim friends, who helped them and their children remain anchored in their Islamic faith, Iranian culture, and morals.

A Movement Begins

Shortly after arriving in the new country, they met an Iranian couple, Dina and Omar. Amal was drawn to Dina, noticing something "wonderfully different" about her that she could not explain. She hoped they would become close friends—that is, until Dina disclosed something that surprised and shocked Amal: Dina and Omar were no longer Muslim; they had become Christians.

Amal had known a few Christians in Iran, but they had not

interacted with her on any meaningful level, and they had never shared their Christian faith. In Iran, seeking to convert Muslims into Christians is illegal. Amal had heard of Christians breaking that law. Those people typically disappeared, either killed or imprisoned. Amal thought the law was just and necessary to protect weak Muslims from being lured away into hell. Amal also believed Iran was doing the right thing by living out the "there is no compulsion in religion" quote from the Quran, allowing nonevangelistic Christians to live in her country in peace.

Dumfounded by Dina's confession, Amal didn't know how to respond. Suddenly, she saw Dina as a lawbreaker—a weak soul who had been lured into darkness and might attempt to drag her away from her Muslim faith as well. Amal wanted to say something to Dina, do anything to save her; instead, distraught and filled with fear, Amal abruptly ended the conversation with Dina, asking her to never again contact her family.

Concerned for their own family, Amal and Ali prayed and looked for ways they could protect themselves and their children from being lured away from Islam as Omar and Dina's family had been. But Amal had one question for Dina: Why?

The Spark That Ignited It

The question haunted Amal. After a few months, Amal felt compelled to know the answer. With Ali's full knowledge, Amal contacted Dina. For the first time in her life, Amal heard the good news of Jesus Christ as she listened to Dina's testimony. In summary, a Western Christian, Joanna, had shared her faith with Dina, and after a period of studying the Bible and praying, Dina and her family accepted Christ as Lord and Savior.

Before they parted ways, Dina offered Amal a Bible so she could read the good news for herself and examine whether the Bible is truly God's uncorrupted word. Amal accepted. Then Dina asked to pray with Amal so that God could reveal the truth to her. Again, Amal accepted.

Amal then studied the Bible daily, always praying for God to reveal the truth to her. And daily, Amal shared what she learned with her husband, Ali. After six months of prayer and Bible study, Amal came to believe that Jesus is God's Son, and she accepted Him as her Lord and Savior. A few days later, Ali did the same. Within a few months, so did their children.

After that, Ali and Amal felt convicted that they must tell all their family and relatives in Iran about the good news (the gospel) of Jesus Christ. They believed they needed to do so in person because they believed the government monitored all communications into Iran, and they did not want to put their loved ones at risk.

The Return to Iran

With that in mind, Ali and Amal traveled back to Iran with the intention of sharing about Jesus with their families and relatives. They believed the government would closely watch them, so they had to share the gospel secretly and quickly before they were discovered.

They snuck Bibles into the country and gave them away to their family and friends. They shared the good news with dozens of loved ones and prayed with them, asking God to reveal His truth. Many accepted Jesus as their personal Lord and Savior.

Within days, Amal and Ali were arrested.

Ali and Amal were aware that they could lose everything, including their lives. They knew that nonevangelistic Christians lived in Iran at peace, just as they typically have in most Islamic countries throughout the history of Islam. But eyewitness reports from people (Iranians, foreigners living there, Christians, Muslims, and Christians from Muslim background) who lived in Iran through 2010 reported intense persecution of evangelistic Christians, especially of former Iranian Muslims, even to the point of death.

Before returning to Iran to share their new faith, Amal and

Ali considered the reality that they could very well face similar persecution. They knew they might be given the choices that ISIS or other radical Islamic groups had imposed on Christians in their territories:

- They could denounce their Christian faith and convert to Islam.
- They could pay a special fee to be allowed to live there as non-evangelistic Christians, keeping their faith private
- They could face the possibility of persecution, even death.[29]

Amal and Ali committed to each other that they would not denounce their faith or pay the fee and keep the good news to themselves. They determined they would share their new faith for as long as they were alive. It was a risky decision, but they chose to not allow the fear of what people might do to them from stopping them from obeying (by being evangelistic) and trusting God with their lives.

When they were arrested, Ali and Amal were indeed given a choice to face severe consequences or denounce their newfound Christian faith and convert back to Islam. They refused to deny Christ at any cost.

The Real Treasure

The authorities seized all their assets, which included properties, investments, money, and business holdings. But Ali and Amal were surprised (and relieved) that their lives were spared. Rather that imprisoning the couple, the government deported them.

Amal and Ali lost all of earthly assets, but they told me, "We, and

[29] "Syria Crisis: ISIS imposes rules on Christians in Raqqa," *BBC News*, Feb. 27, 2014, http://www.bbc.com/news/world-middle-east-26366197.http://www.bbc.com/news/world-middle-east-26366197.

many of our relatives, gained Jesus—our eternal treasure that no one can take away. That was worth it!"

To Ali and Amal and the dozens they led to Christ, "The kingdom of heaven is like a merchant in search of fine pearls, who, on finding one pearl of great value, went and sold all that he had and bought it" (Matthew 13:45–46 ESV).

The Impact of One Faithful Witness

This story began with Joanna. When Omar and Dina moved into Joanna's neighborhood, she befriended them and eventually shared the good news of Jesus with them.

That sparked a chain reaction. First, Dina and Omar and their family accepted Christ as their Lord and Savior. Then Dina shared the gospel with Amal, who shared it with Ali. Then their children became believers in Christ. When Ali and Amal went back to Iran to share the gospel, dozens of their extended family members and friends also put their faith in Jesus as Lord and Savior.

In the past few years, approximately three hundred seventy thousand people from Muslim backgrounds in Iran have become Christians.[30] Joanna had a role in that, even though she has never been to Iran. But she shared the gospel with a friend in her neighborhood (Dina). It was an act that ignited a global chain reaction that resulted in new believers in Iran.

Three hundred seventy thousand is an amazingly high number given the history of persecution of evangelistic Christians in Iran. Until recently, almost all Christians living in Iran were non-evangelistic; they lived in fear of what might happen to them if they shared their faith with Muslims.

In recent years, things appear to be changing in Iran. A variety of factors have contributed to this change, with the love of Christ being

[30] Aghajanian, Liana, "Iran's Oppressed Christians," *The New York Times,* March 14, 2014, http://www.nytimes.com/2014/03/15/opinion/irans-oppressed-christians.html.

the main catalyst. The main change is that believers like Amal and Ali are stepping out in daring faith to obey God instead of man, and more Iranian Muslims are discovering the truth of the gospel.

Today Amal, Ali, and their children live in a Christianized nation and are alumni of iHOPE trainings. They are ambassadors for Christ, working alongside other iHOPE alumni to share the good news of Jesus with the Muslims God brings to their city. Because of people like Ali and Amal, many Muslims have become followers of Christ, and these new Christians formed churches where they can worship in their native languages.

This amazing movement began with one Christian, crossing cultural, language, and religious lines to share the gospel with a Muslim living in her local area. The result was a powerful *glocal* impact that continues to transform lives today.

One Couple's Impact on the Arab/Israeli Conflict

Like many people living outside of the MENA region, Renee and Jack felt saddened as they watched the news of the ongoing conflicts between Palestinians and Israelis, Muslims, and Jews. They personally loved the Jewish people and the nation of Israel, and from a political perspective, they sided with Israel against Palestinian groups like Hamas or the Palestinian Liberation Organization (PLO).

From a spiritual perspective, however, they were filled with God's love for both people groups, Palestinians and Israelis. They felt God calling them to leave the comfort and safety of their Christianized nation and move to minister to Palestinians. They did not know if their efforts would make much of an impact with the people, the area, or the conflict, but they determined to obey God. Their motto was, "Simply obey God and trust Him with the results."

Jack and Renee moved to an Arabic country to work with an evangelistic Christian group that had a ministry in poverty-stricken areas of Palestine. They hoped that, if they shared the love of Christ, some Palestinians would turn to Jesus, and His love would replace the anger or hate they felt toward Israel. Ultimately, they hoped to help, in whatever small measure they could, decrease attacks on Jews. Part of their ministry was teaching children and young people about Jesus, giving away Bibles, and developing friendships through fun and games.

Potential Palestinian Terrorist

Muslim parents sent their children to the retail facility that operated like a neighborhood after-school activity center by the Christian group. The Muslim parents realized that the Christians had "Christian" activities for their Muslim children. But they approved sending them there because it was a physically safer environment for their Muslim children, and there they were less likely to meet an Islamic extremist who may try to recruit them into becoming potential terrorists. One of these teens, Hameed, was a terribly angry Muslim Palestinian boy who constantly got into fights. He had never met his father and wasn't sure if he had abandoned his family or had died fighting in the Palestinian/Israeli Conflict. Some thought Hameed was destined to die in that conflict. Hameed's mom hoped sending him to Jack and Renee would save her son from that fate.

It did. After about five years of Bible study at Jack and Renee's youth programs, Hameed accepted Jesus Christ as Lord and Savior. After that, Hameed earned a college degree and became a successful businessman. He married Ester, and they have a beautiful family.

Swords to Plowshares

Eventually Ester and Hameed realized God had prepared him in unique ways for ministry. They took a big step of daring faith and went into evangelistic ministry full time. They began four years ago by holding church in an apartment in an Islamic city.

Now they lead churches and ministries in several Islamic nations. Hundreds of Muslims from various nationalities, including

Palestinians, are now discipling and multiplying followers of Jesus as Lord and Savior as a result of Hameed's ministries. These potential enemies of the state of Israel, including Hameed himself, have turned their "swords into plowshares" (Isaiah 2:4). They continue to be fruitful and multiply daily.

Hameed is now also a sought-after speaker, traveling throughout the world into Christianized nations to inspire them to share the gospel with Muslims.

It all began with Renee and Jack taking a daring step of faithful obedience to be fruitful and multiply with the gospel.

Reconciled to Reconcile

Jack and Renee did not pursue a ministry in a foreign country because they had human love for Palestinians or Muslims; rather, the presence of God's love in their hearts compelled them to uproot their lives and teach the Bible to children in a country and culture far from home. When they began their faithful journey, they had no idea it would impact thousands for the kingdom, but they knew God had reconciled them so that He might reconcile others through them. He loved them, and they wanted to share that love with others. So when their Palestinian Muslim friends ask why they are willing to risk so much, their answer is simple: "Christ's love compels us."

> For Christ's love compels us, because we are convinced that one died for all, and therefore all died. And he died for all, that those who live should no longer live for themselves but for him who died for them and was raised again. (2 Corinthians 5:14–15 NIV)

Positive and Negative Motivators

God inspires us in incredibly positive ways through His word, with His love and presence in our lives, and with the evidence of His work *in* us as the Holy Spirit helps us develop godly traits of love, goodness, kindness, gentleness, patience, and self-control so we might fulfill His purpose for our lives. In fact, 2 Corinthians 5:14 succinctly explains that His love is a positive motivator that inspires us to be used as instruments of reconciliation.

If you're a parent, however, you know that positive motivation, though powerful, isn't always enough to elicit the kind of behavior you want to see in your child. Negative motivation (or consequences) is often necessary. God supplies that consequence-driven motivation for us as well to inspire us to get involved in His mission. We see that in 2 Corinthians 5:10–11 (NLT): "For we must all stand before Christ to be judged. We will each receive whatever we deserve for the good or evil we have done in this earthly body. Because we understand our fearful responsibility to the Lord, we work hard to persuade others."

With the consequence clearly outlined, the passage then moves on to the positive motivator: "for the love of Christ compels us." God uses both the positive and negative motivators to inspire us to join His mission. Second Corinthians 5:18–20 (NLT) describes God's mission for us this way: "God has given us this task of reconciling people to him. For God was in Christ, reconciling the world to himself ... And He gave us this wonderful message of reconciliation. We are Christ's ambassadors; God is making his appeal through us. We speak for Christ when we plead, 'Come back to God!'"

When Renee and Jack decided to move into the middle of the Arab/Israeli Conflict zone, their loved ones in their Christianized nation strongly objected. They asked questions like "Why would you risk everything, *including your lives*, to do something like that?"

Renee and Jack's consistent reply was that, even if they were heavily persecuted or killed, it was worth it. They justified the earthly risks with verses like 2 Corinthians 4:16–18 (NLT):

> That is why we never give up. Though our bodies are dying, our spirits are being renewed every day. For our present troubles are small and won't last

> very long. Yet they produce for us a glory that vastly outweighs them and will last forever! So we don't look at the troubles we can see now; rather, we fix our gaze on things that cannot be seen. For the things we see now will soon be gone, but the things we cannot see will last forever.

Why should anyone leave comfort, safety, pleasure, and happiness to risk everything so that the light of the gospel shines through them? Because God tells us in verses like these not to focus our lives on present earthly things that we can see and touch. Those things are temporary, and they will be gone soon; rather, we are to join Him in His mission to reconcile humanity to Himself. With that mission as our focus, we gain rewards that will last for eternity.

Renee and Jack chose to take a long-term view of fulfillment and success. More Christians need to do the same. We need to be actively involved in being fruitful and multiplying by expanding the spiritual family of our eternally loving Father. On one hand, the people who need to hear about Jesus depend on our willingness to go into all the nations. On the other hand, our future generations need us to model for them how to prioritize our lives so God's mission is first. They will see us living out the desire to see "His kingdom come, His will be done" in our daily lives—not just in church and at Bible study. They need to see us abiding in the Branch and proving we are His disciples by being fruitful. The future of our cities, countries, and world and the fate of generations to come depends on our willingness to obey God and fulfill His mission; likewise, how God judges us for eternity also depends on the actions we take today.

Know that God holds us accountable and will ask each of us, "What did you do with all the talent, resources, and time I gave you?" God wants to see that we used them, invested them, and as a result fulfilled His purpose for us by being fruitful and multiplying His kingdom.

So whether the fear of the Lord drives you or the love of Christ compels you—or perhaps *both* fear and love stir your heart—go share the message of reconciliation with which God has entrusted you.

A History of Failure

A main contributing factor to our Islamic problem is not a new one; in fact, we can see the full cycle of this issue at play in the Old Testament book of Judges, not with Christians and Muslims, of course, but with God, His people, and their neglect to follow His commands. The book of Judges spans approximately four hundred years of Israel's history. Like Christians today, Israel (the nation) had been redeemed and God had established a special relationship with His people.

But Israel repeatedly failed to live the way God wanted them to—just like others before them had and as many Christians continue to do today. One of Israel's recurring failures was prioritizing other things (idols, wealth, personal desires) above God. As a result, they wasted the gifts and resources God had given them, using them to pursue their own priorities rather than fulfil God's purpose for their lives.

In Judges 4, we learn that Israel had disobeyed God and was consequently being oppressed by a wicked king. Those who were faithful to God cried out for help and followed His direction to revolt against that king. In doing so, they risked everything—some paying with their lives—to obey God and free the nation of Israel. Because of their faithful obedience, God provided an awesome victory over their oppressors.

In Judges 5, we see a victory song that records the faithful obedience—even unto death—of those who had trusted and obeyed God and joined Him in His mission. The song also records the names of the tribes who did not trust God or follow Him into battle.

> Among the clans of Reuben there was much searching of heart. Why did you sit still among the sheepfolds, to hear the whistling for the flocks? Among the

> clans of Reuben there was much searching of heart.
> (Judges 5:15–16 NIV)

The tribe of Reuben was the size of a small nation. It was big and powerful, yet its people chose not to join in God's mission. Instead, in language that is a fit for today's world, they stayed home to tend to their businesses. Perhaps as they searched their hearts, they thought about going to help in the battle. They may have considered strategies and debated about whether the risks were worth their time and effort. In the end, however, they determined they were too busy at home, so they decided against the sacrifice required to join God's mission.

Judges 5:17 continues with the addition of three more tribes to this hall of shame: "Gilead stayed beyond the Jordan. And Dan, why did he linger by the ships? Asher remained on the coast and stayed in his coves."

Gilead, descendants of the family of beloved Joseph, also decided not to join God's mission. The families of Dan and Asher did not join either. They disobeyed God, pursuing their selfish interests and purposes rather than fulfilling their most relevant purpose. Like Ruben, these three tribes were financially well off. Going into battle meant putting their lives and resources at stake, and they decided it was too great a risk; instead, they stayed active in their businesses and enjoyed spending their money on nice homes, comfort, safety, and recreation.

The Bible reveals that the tribes of Ruben, Gilead, Dan, and Asher continued to live out this kind of self-focus and self-preservation. As a result, these tribes, along with six others, eventually disappeared. They are remembered as the lost ten tribes of Israel.

Repeating History

When Islam sprang up in the Middle East and North Africa, many Christians behaved much like the four tribes mentioned in Judges 5:15–17. They disobeyed God and refused to join His mission, counting the cost as too great. They chose not to share the gospel with Muslims; they stopped being fruitful and multiplying God's kingdom. As a result, Christianity in that region all but disappeared. Like the lost ten tribes of Israel, they got lost in history. The region entrusted to them went from being Christianized to almost completely Muslim.

History continues to repeat itself in today's Christianized nations where God's redeemed people are responding in almost the same way the four tribes in Judges 5:15–17 did. The following statistics, one regarding human resources and the other regarding financial resources, reveal a troubling similarity in mindset and inaction.

Regarding human resources, in 2001, 5.52 million Christians served in full-time ministry worldwide. Most of them—5,489,300 people—worked in the Christian or evangelized world, serving around 2.5 billion people. That means 99.44 percent of all Christian workers and missionaries served in the evangelized and Christianized world while only 30,500 Christians served in full-time ministry in the un-evangelized and unreached world, which represented around 3.6 billion people. A mere half of 1 percent of all Christian ministry is done in the unevangelized areas among the world's unreached people.

Regarding financial resources, in 2001, Christians gave $270 billion in annual income to their churches and to missionary organizations. Of that total, $269.75 billion, or 99.9991 percent, was invested in the evangelized and Christianized areas, containing around 2.5 billion people.

That means 250 million, or a mere 0.0009 percent, was invested in the unevangelized and unreached world, containing around 3.6 billion people.[31]

As of the writing of this book, it appears that all these above percentages have not changed much, if any.

Whether by ignorance or intentional neglect, we are not (at least

---

[31] David Barrett and Todd Johnson, "Global Document 24," *World Christian Trends,* (William Carey Library, 2013), http://www.gordonconwell.edu/ockenga/research/documents/gd24.pdf.

not in great enough numbers) following God into spiritual "battle" by giving of our time, lives, or financial resources to reach the unreached. Like the lost ten tribes of Israel, we often prefer to remain in the safety and comfort of our homes, tending to our families and businesses and perhaps sharing the gospel with those we are most like. In short, we are repeating the biblical and historical cycles of failing to adequately fulfill God's second primary purpose for our lives.

I pray that as more Christians become aware of how neglecting to spread the gospel negatively affects entire nations, we will all—as individuals, churches, and ministries—focus on inspiring, equipping, and prayerfully and financially supporting Christians to *go* as Jesus commanded and join God in His mission to draw *all* people to Himself.

You can be part of the solution. Start a conversation in your church, and let others know of the severe consequences of failing to fulfil God's purpose for our lives. Together we can join God's mission and turn things around—for the sake of our families, our communities, and our world for the generations to come.

The Only Way You Can Be Fruitful

There are five essentials for every Christian to know and do to be faithful to God's commands and maximize fruitfulness. All five are very interconnected. We know that the first thing is the sharing of the good news (the gospel) about Jesus as Lord and Savior. We will cover the other four in the coming chapters. For now, let us remember a very foundational condition for all five to work effectively and for you to be fruitful and multiply: abide.

Abiding in Jesus means to continue in ongoing relationship with Him. An abiding relationship with God includes the following:

- Read the Bible regularly to get to know God better as He reveals Himself through His word.

- Pray (talk to and listen to God), asking God to help you understand what you are reading and what He wants you to know and do and to reveal His will for us. A summary of God's will for you in the Bible is to be in a relationship with Him and be "fruitful and multiply."
- Worship God. As we get to know God and pray, we want to worship Him.
- Obey God by doing what He is asking you to do as revealed in His word, in prayer, and in worship.

A Personal Benefit to Being Fruitful

Being obedient to God has many benefits, and one that is highlighted in this passage is found in John 15:11 (ESV): "That your *joy* may be full."

Every person (including myself) in every story I have shared and will share in this book who is being fruitful and multiplying is experiencing ongoing and abiding joy. I did not experience lasting peace or joy in my personal life until I began to abide in Jesus and became fruitful.

God is not dependent on us to produce fruit. God can save all the lost, everyone in the world, and all Muslims without us or our participation. But God has been inviting believers throughout history—including you right now—to join Him in His work of redemption. If you answer the call of this most blessed opportunity to abide and be fruitful, you will experience enduring joy and peace that comes from helping Muslims (and the lost in general) find and follow Jesus.

Being fruitful is the evidence/proof that you are abiding in and following Jesus. And as we read in this chapter, it can be remarkably simple. Joanna, Jack and Renee, Dina and Omar, Amal and Ali all loved on Muslims, shared their faith with them, gave them Bibles, and prayed with them in the name of Jesus. They are all fruitful and multiplying, contributing to the harvest with thousands of Muslims accepting Jesus as Lord and Savior and who also are now multiplying disciples.

CHAPTER 7
The Muslim Worldview

The first of the five essentials for every Christian to know and do is to be part of God's redemption plan by being fruitful and multiplying spiritually. For the kingdom of God to have a harvest of souls, each of us needs to be part of the mission to plant gospel seeds by sharing the message of Christ as Lord and Savior.

Any gardener or farmer knows that a fruitful harvest begins with understanding the soil where you are planting seeds. The specific soil we're working with—the soil that so desperately needs those gospel seeds—is the heart and mind of a Muslim.

What's challenging is that Christians worldwide, and especially Western Christians, are not familiar with Muslim culture. I have had thousands of Christians approach me with comments like "I don't understand Muslims!" and "Since I don't understand Muslims well, I am afraid to offend them with what I say or do." Often these become insurmountable obstacles in the minds of Christians, demotivating them from even planting gospel seeds with Muslims.

Maybe you can relate. If so, you certainly aren't alone. The Islamic religion and its followers can seem like a complex, complicated puzzle to solve. My challenge to you is to not allow fear and uncertainty to prevent you from sharing the truth of Christ with Muslims.

Understanding the Muslim Worldview

As with anything, a little knowledge and a generous spirit of love can help you overcome those obstacles. To help you, my goal in this chapter is to simplify what seems complex and to help you solve this puzzle. It is far simpler than you may believe. It does not require a college degree in cross-cultural communication or Islamic studies. After this chapter, you will have the relevant and foundational information you need to have a better understanding of the Islamic worldview and Muslims, how they think and feel, and why they do much of what they do.

Understanding the Muslim worldview will help you do the following.

- You will understand why every Christian needs to know and do the five essentials that are the main subject of this book.
- You will know how to apply these essentials with Muslims.
- You will understand why these simple actions are so effective with Muslims.
- It will help you shape conversations and relationships with Muslims.
- You will comprehend the vast differences between the Christian and Muslim worldviews.

Eureka!

Todd has a theological degree from a seminary and a degree in Islamic studies. He shepherds a church in an area of a Christianized nation where hundreds of thousands of Muslims have immigrated either to attend university or because they are displaced refugees. Todd has a heart for Muslims and serves with mission projects worldwide that work with Muslims.

Todd had been faithfully reaching out to Muslims for three years when he attended one of our equipping workshops. Before the workshop began, I greeted him, and knowing about his personal experience with Muslims and his educational background, I asked Todd why he came to our workshop.

Todd answered, "I want to have a better understanding of Muslims. I still don't understand Muslims and some of the things they do."

After the workshop was over, Todd ran to me and said, "I now understand Muslims! I've had more *aha* moments in the past three hours than I've had in the previous three years."

Islamic Denominations

To understand Muslims more clearly, it is helpful to begin by looking at Christianity's main branches and various denominations. The vast majority of Christian churches can be organized into two major branches: Protestant or Catholic. Of course, there are many different denominations under each major branch. Under the Protestant category, for example, there are Baptists, Evangelicals, Lutherans, Methodists, Pentecostal, Presbyterian, and many others. Each of these Protestant denominations has its own varieties; for example, under Baptist denominations, there are free will, reformed, Southern, and many others.

What differentiates these major Christian branches and denominations are theological (theology is the study of God and His nature and of religious beliefs) views on certain issues. Some churches, for example, believe in baptizing infants; others do not.

What unites all these denominations as *Christian* are the theological views they share in common. For example, Christian denominations assert and believe in the virgin birth of Christ, that Jesus was crucified for our sins, that He was buried and rose again, and that we must accept Jesus as Lord and Savior.

For all the differences between Christian denominations, these core, common beliefs are the foundation for the Christian worldview.

Like Christianity, Islam has two major branches: Sunni (about 85 percent of Muslims) or Shiites (about 15 percent). Within those two major branches, Muslims fall into diverse groups (denominations). For example, under the Sunni category are the Salafi, Wahhabi, and other distinct groups.

A main differentiator between Sunnis and Shiites is the question of who the appropriate leader of Islam was/is after the death of Muhammad. The difference of opinion on this matter comes with strong thoughts and feelings on both sides, and had even led to war between the two branches.

Just as it is with Christian denominations, both branches of Islam share similar, essential doctrines and beliefs. In the next three sections, we'll examine the common beliefs shared by all Muslims of all denominations worldwide. Please note that this is an overview—not a comprehensive study on Islam—and it will give you the basics you need to know to understand the Muslim worldview.

Muhammad Founded Islam

Islam was founded by Muhammad, and all Muslims consider him a holy prophet and the last messenger God will ever send to humankind.

Islam teaches that Muhammad received revelations from God between AD 610 until he died at age sixty-two in AD 632. These revelations from God form the text of the Quran, Islam's holy book and central religious text. In addition to the Quran, Muhammad's teachings and practices are written in the Hadith and Sira, which are accepted by Muslims as religious literature to guide their lives and laws.

Six Major Islamic Beliefs

Muslims share six beliefs that come from the Quran, Hadith, and Sira:

1. *Belief in oneness of God.* Like Christians, Muslims believe that God is the Creator of all things and that God is all-powerful

and all-knowing. Unlike Christians, Muslims do not believe in the triune God (the Trinity as God the Father, the Son, and the Holy Spirit).

2. *Belief in angels.* Like Christians, Muslims believe angels exist as unseen beings who worship God and carry out His orders throughout the universe.
3. *Belief in the books of God.* Muslims believe that God revealed holy books to a number of God's messengers. This includes but is not limited to: the Torah, given to Moses; the Psalms given to David; the scrolls given to Abraham; and the gospel given to Jesus. But Muslims believe that all other original scriptures were somehow changed, and that is why God revealed the Quran to the prophet Muhammad. They believe that the Quran is the only text that remains in its original form, and as such, Muslims accept only the Quran as scripture. So Muslims typically accept, read, and follow the Quran but don't read the Holy Bible (Old or New Testament).
4. *Belief in the prophets or messengers of God.* Muslims believe God's guidance has been revealed to humankind through specially appointed prophets throughout history, beginning with the first man, Adam, who is considered the first prophet. Twenty-five of these prophets are mentioned by name in the Quran, including Noah, Abraham, and Moses. Unlike Christians, Muslims do not believe in the deity of Jesus. They consider Him to be a prophet and messenger from God. Muslims believe Muhammad is the last in this line of prophets/messengers, sent for all humankind with the message of Islam.
5. *Belief in the Day of Judgment.* Muslims believe that on the Day of Judgment, humans will be judged for their actions in this life. Those who followed God's guidance are more likely to be rewarded with paradise, but salvation is not guaranteed; meanwhile, those who reject God's guidance will likely be

punished with hell. God is sovereign, and He chooses those on whom He will have mercy and allow into paradise.

6. *Belief in the divine decree.* Muslims believe that everything that happens in one's life is preordained as part of God's will. A Muslim must respond to the good and the bad with a positive and wise attitude. God's will does not negate human free will, so humans are still responsible for their choices and responses to whatever happens.

Five Pillars of Islam

Muslims are expected to put the above six major beliefs into action in their daily lives. The way they do so is through the five pillars of Islam. These pillars constitute the core, the to-do actions of the Islamic faith.

1. *Shahada. Shahada* means "witness" or "testimony." *Shahada* is a Muslim's declaration of faith. The *Shahada* is the most fundamental belief of Islam: "There is no god but Allah, and Muhammad is the messenger of Allah." (*Allah* is God in Arabic.) To convert to Islam, one must believe and make this statement. The first part of the statement affirms Islam's monotheism. The second half of the statement affirms the belief that Muhammad is not only a prophet but a messenger of God, a role previously held by Moses (God's messenger to the Jews), Jesus (God's messenger to Christians), and now Muhammad (God's messenger with the message to the entire human race, past, present, and future). The second half of the statement is essential to the Muslim belief that Muhammad is the final vehicle of revelation from God.
2. *Salat.* This word means prayer. Muslims are expected to pray five times per day. The times are daybreak, noon, midafternoon, sunset, and evening. Part of the goal of daily ritual prayers is to serve as an ongoing reminder throughout

the day to keep focused on God amid daily life and all it entails.

3. *Zakat.* This word means charity or offering (like tithing for Christians). Muslims are required to contribute 2.5 percent of their total wealth and assets (not just income) annually. The Quran instructs that Muslims give the Zakat to "the cause of Allah" (could be mosque or Islamic outreach ministries) and to the poor and needy (could be Islamic charities).
4. *Annual fast of Ramadan. Ramadan* is the ninth month in the Islamic calendar. The month refers to the time in which Muhammad first received revelations from God. Muslims are required to fast from food, drink, and sexual activity from sunrise to sunset in observance of this holy month. The purpose of this time of fasting is to focus on spiritual goals and disciplines. The end of the month is celebrated with family gatherings, feasts, and gift giving.
5. *Hajj.* This word means pilgrimage. A pilgrimage to Mecca in Saudi Arabia is expected to be completed at least once in the lifetime of every Muslim who is physically and financially able. Muslims believe Mecca is home to the first house of worship of God, said to have been built by Abraham and his son Ishmael. Muslims worldwide face Mecca when they pray.

Jesus: The Essential Difference between Christianity and Islam

The main point of differentiation between Islam and Christianity centers around the identity, nature, and role of Jesus Christ. Christians believe that Jesus Christ is God. In Islam, Jesus is not.

As Christians, we believe Jesus came to earth as the Son of God. In Islam, Jesus is a messenger (a highly respected position and title for a human, but not divine) who was sent by God to point people back to the one true God.

Christians believe salvation is achieved only through the death and resurrection of Jesus Christ. Only Jesus's sacrificial death on the cross meets God's perfect standard of holiness, love, grace, and justice. God guarantees salvation to anyone who submits his or her life to and accepts Jesus as Lord and Savior. One either rejects God's free gift of salvation in Jesus or accepts it through Him. There is no other way for humans to gain salvation.[32]

In Islam, the cross is not necessary, as only Allah saves by his mercy as he chooses to forgive whom he chooses to forgive. Muslims work hard (through the five pillars and six beliefs) to please Allah, hoping he will choose to forgive them on Judgment Day.

Christians believe salvation is guaranteed to those who believe that Jesus is the Son of God and trust Him as their Savior. In Islam, to claim Jesus is the Son of God guarantees loss of salvation, as it is an unforgiveable sin and blasphemy to add "partners" to the one and only Allah.

The one thing that differentiates Christianity from Islam—and from all other religions or belief systems in the world—is what one believes about Jesus Christ and how one responds to Him.

Islam's Primary Purpose

In summary, Islam believes that God's original revelations written in the Christian Bible have been changed. As a result, Muslims believe that Christianity has strayed from monotheism, from the one true God, Creator of everything, the God of Abraham, and Christians now worship a false god we describe as the Trinity. They operate from the belief that Allah gave the complete and final revelation to Muhammad (the Quran). With that in mind, one main purpose of Islam is to bring humankind back to God's one and true revelation by pointing everyone to the one true Allah (beliefs one and three from the six beliefs of Islam). By guiding the world to become Muslim, they

---

[32] Please examine the Bible to verify the above paragraph. You may begin with verses in John 3:18 and 14:6; Acts 4:11–12; Romans 3:21–26 and 10:9–11; and 1 John 5:12.

will have fulfilled God's second primary purpose for humankind: to be fruitful and multiply.

Islam's Primary Goal

Islam's main goal is to help establish and usher in the kingdom of God on earth.

Throughout history, Muslim scholars, clergy, leaders, politicians, and individuals have disagreed about what this goal entails and how to accomplish it. This is one reason there are different denominations within Islam.

So why do Muslims disagree so much about the details surrounding Islam's main goal?

As you consider this important question, think about it in terms of Christians and Christianity. Historically (and still today), Christian scholars, clergy, leaders, politicians, and individuals have disagreed about many things. This is a reason there are different denominations within Christianity. For a Christian example, consider the end-time prophecies found throughout the Bible, especially in the book of Revelation. What do these prophecies mean? What should we do about them? There are widespread disagreements on the interpretations and answers to those two questions among Christians, scholars, clergy, leaders, and politicians. Moreover, I have seen heated debates about this (and other issues) between Christians within the same denomination—within the same local church! The way people answer questions about such issues forms their views, which inform their actions.

Let's turn back to the main Islamic questions of this section: *What does the kingdom of Allah look like, and how does Islam help usher it in and establish it on earth?* Let's explore these questions and the different Muslim viewpoints to help gain better understanding of the Muslim worldview.

The Muslim Worldview of Old Testament Israel and Christianity

We'll begin with the seven similarities between the Islamic and Old Testament Israel worldviews. For all the differences between Islam and Christianity, it is possible to find some common ground that can open the door for Bible study.

1. The One True God

In Genesis, the first book of the Bible, we learn that God created Adam and Eve to be His people, and He would be their God. Humankind then sinned, shattering their fellowship with one another as well as with God. That trajectory away from God continued until only one man, Noah (Genesis 6:8–9), walked with the one true God. Humankind had become so evil that God brought the flood, and only Noah's family remained on earth. God was to be their God, and they were to be His people.

As the population grew, humankind strayed from the one true God again, creating idols and worshiping multiple gods. Then God called Abraham and promised to grow his family into a great nation (Israel). God promised to bless all nations of the earth through them. God was Abraham's God, and Abraham's family were His people.

By the second book of the Bible, Abraham's descendants (now known as the Israelites) had grown to exceptionally large numbers and were enslaved in Egypt. But God rescued the Israelites from Egypt. The nation of Israel agreed to be God's people, and He would be their God. But again (and again) Israel fell into the same old sinful pattern of straying from God. The Israelites made idols and fell into polytheism by worshiping other gods.

Islam teaches that Old Testament Israel, as a nation and a people, failed in their duty to point the world away from polytheism and back to the one true God. Muslims believe that this failure is the reason Allah sent Jesus as the new messenger who would point people to the one true God. Christianity, then, was to continue in that role and turn the world away from polytheism.

But just as Old Testament Israel failed throughout history, so did Christianity. Even Christians, in the Islamic view, fell into polytheism by elevating Jesus from the highest possible human position of messenger or prophet, into deity as the Son of God.

Islam does not understand the Trinity or the concept of a triune God. Triune means three in one, as in the Father, Son, and Holy Spirit—one God, three divine Persons. Many Muslims misunderstand the Christian belief of the Trinity, and they view it as Christians worshiping three different gods rather than the one true God.

In the Islamic view, the world has once again strayed from the one true God and fallen into polytheism. Because Old Testament Israel and Christianity failed to turn away from polytheism, Muslims now are to serve as Allah's instrument to guide people to worship the one true God.

2. God's Holy Word

Islam believes that God gave His word to Old Testament Israel and to Christians. But they believe that somehow the scriptures have been corrupted, leading Jews astray and resulting in Christians having a distorted view of God (such as the Trinity doctrine), His laws, and His primary purposes.

Muslims believe that God gave His word to Muhammad, which was recorded in the Quran, where God promised to protect His eternal word. They believe God has given each Muslim a part in the work of spreading His truth to point a lost world back to the one true God and His word (the Quran).

How the Above Aspects of the Muslim Worldview May Affect You

The following is a story that illustrates a common response of Muslims to friendships formed with Christians. It reveals how the Muslim worldview can impact relationships you may have with Muslims.

Samir and Sheba are a young married Muslim couple. They were born and raised in an Islamic country, where they had never been befriended by a Christian, nor had they heard the gospel. They knew their faith well and considered themselves good, moral Muslims who wanted to please God. Samir was pursuing a college degree in science, while Sheba was studying to become a doctor.

Since birth, Samir and Sheba had heard that Western nations were Christian and that Christianity is a false religion with corrupted scriptures. They were taught that Christians were immoral, sinning against God in many ways and engaging in the worst sin of all: the idolatry of worshiping false gods. They were also taught that Christian nations, especially America, were in some ways political and military enemies of Islam and Muslims.

Even believing this, Samir and Sheba wanted to go to the United States, where they could receive a superior education. Their parents and relatives were supportive of the idea of Samir and Sheba pursuing opportunities to get their college degrees in America if they remained grounded in their Islamic faith and true to the one and only God.

Samir and Sheba were thrilled when they were accepted into a university in the United States and granted visas as international students. Even in their excitement, Sheba and Samir were fearful about living in a "spiritually dark" Christian country.

When they arrived in the United States, they rented a room from a Christian American couple, Jane and Norm, who lived close to the university. Like most other Muslim students coming from an Islamic country, even though Samir and Sheba were a little scared at first, they embraced the opportunity to live with Christians. Muslim international students typically desire to live with natives of the country where they're studying. They believe this will help them learn the local language much quicker. So in this case, Samir and Sheba believed they'd learn good English more quickly if they were living with Americans. Due to their fears of an immoral Western society, Muslim international students like Samir and Sheba prefer to live with Christians who appear more moral than others.

Sheba and Samir felt loved by Norm and Jane in a way that was completely unfamiliar to them. Unlike anything they had experienced, this love shattered the negative perceptions Samir and Sheba had about Christians. They quickly grew to love their Christian hosts in return.

Samir and Sheba began to pray for Jane and Norm to become Muslims and hopefully, enter heaven. They believed God was giving them the opportunity to share His true word, so they gave them a Quran as a gift, which their Christian hosts graciously accepted. Sheba and Samir embraced the opportunity to please God by pointing their wonderful but "spiritually misguided" Christian friends back to the one and only true God.

Jane and Norm saw Samir and Sheba's sincerity—and believed wholeheartedly that they were sincerely wrong in their Islamic faith. After accepting the gift of the Quran, Jane and Norm gave Samir and Sheba a study Bible, which they graciously accepted. Eventually, Norm and Jane invited Samir and Sheba to church with them, and they went. There, they heard the gospel for the first time.

The story of Sheba and Samir is ongoing as of this writing. They have joined a Bible study and are continuing to learn about God and salvation through Jesus.

My experience, and that of hundreds of other Christians who have shared their stories with me, is that Muslims typically reach out in a caring manner (not an antagonistic one) once Christians befriend them. Many Muslims desire to share what they believe is God's true word (the Quran) and help point you back to the one and only true God (the God of Islam). Their hope is that God will save you in His mercy.

3. God's Nation on Earth

The third similarity between the Old Testament nation of Israel and the Islamic worldview is that Islam believes that as God's chosen nation, they are to be light in a spiritually dark world.

Islam teaches that after God redeemed the people of Israel from Egypt, He established them as His nation on earth. In the Islamic view, there was no separation of religion and government. God established Israel to be a theocracy, a nation where God's directives rule all civil, social, and religious aspects of life. This theocracy was to benefit the entire world. Israel was to be God's people and nation, and He was to be their God and King. Then God would shine His light through Israel as a model nation for the rest of the world.

But Israel rejected God as their King and demanded a human one so they could be like the nations around them. That resulted in Israel failing in their responsibility and eventually forfeiting their special status as God's chosen nation and royal priesthood.

In the Islamic view, Christians failed as well by becoming misguided in the priestly and royal duties God gave them of filling the earth with humans who are righteous. That's when God called Islam as His nation on earth. God gave Islam the responsibility to succeed where Christians and the Old Testament nation of Israel had failed. God expects to rule Islam as one nation on earth, without national boundaries. God gave Islam the responsibility to help establish and usher in the kingdom of God, where the entire world is Muslim, with God as King and Ruler.

With this belief system in mind, it is easier to grasp why Islam, in general, does not embrace the concept of separation of religion and government. Islam views such separation as a rebellion against God. Muslims do not want to repeat the mistake the Old Testament nation of Israel made in seeking freedom from God.

This insight is important because it helps us understand why, when Western nations propose the idea of political (as one example) freedom to Islamic nations, it is viewed as a form of rebellion against

God. It's also why Islam views Western nations—where there is a separation of secular government and religion—in the same sort of light as the pagan nations that surrounded the Old Testament nation of Israel. In the Muslim worldview, secular governments and freedom are Satan's enticements to lure the world away from God.

To recap: God expected Israel to be a model nation and to reject the ways of the pagan nations around them. His intention was for the Israelites to share His light with the nations around them, by revealing and living out God's laws and government. Its people fell in line with the world rather than being instruments of God to attract a wayward world back to the one true God. Muslims believe God appointed that responsibility to Islam in the seventh century, and He expects Islam to succeed where Judaism and Christianity previously failed.

4. God's Holy Law

I've mentioned that, in the Islamic view, God established the Old Testament nation of Israel to be a theocracy ruled by His holy law, governing every area of life. The Ten Commandments were like a constitution to His nation. Then God revealed more of His laws in what Jews and Christians refer to as the Mosaic law of the Old Testament. The law governed their religious life and interactions with God, their human relationships, and their civil and social areas of life.

In the Islamic view, the Old Testament law in Israel was to be a model for the rest of the lawless world, but Israel generally did not abide by God's holy law. Then Christianity claimed that God did away with the law altogether, which is why Islam generally views Christians as misguided people who use their misunderstanding of God's grace as license to sin.

In the Islamic view, God gave His nation, Islam, His holy law, which is now referred to as *Sharia* law. The term *Sharia* means "path" or "way." *Sharia* law is the legal system by which God expects His nation and people to abide. It governs humans' relationship with

God and with each other. Islam expects Islamic nations to abide by *Sharia* law.

In the Islamic worldview, the perfect scenario would be one in which Islam succeeds at ushering in and establishing the kingdom of God on earth. With that mission accomplished, everyone will be Muslim, and Sharia law will be the law of the world, with God as ruler and judge.

Meanwhile, because Christianized nations typically have secular governments with a defined separation of religion and state, their laws are not based on or connected to a specific religion or its holy scriptures. To Islam's dismay, Christianized nations do not abide by the Ten Commandments, Mosaic law, or Sharia law as law of the land, and as such, they set an example that lures the world away from God and His Sharia law.

5. Penal Code

In addition to giving Old Testament Israel the Ten Commandments and Mosaic law, God gave the Israelites a penal code that prescribed the punishments for breaking His holy law. For example, breaking any of the first three commandments (Exodus 20:3–7), which have to do with humanity's relationship with God, constitutes blasphemy. The penalty for blasphemy in the Old Testament was the stoning to death of the blasphemer (Leviticus 24:10–23). Regarding human relations with each other, murder is the violation of the sixth commandment (Exodus 20:13) and was punishable by death (Leviticus 24:17). Committing adultery violates the seventh commandment (Exodus 20:14), and the sin was likewise punishable by death (Leviticus 20:10).

Islam teaches that Sharia law is God's law and that breaking it is sin. Muslims believe God is holy and that He commands humans to be holy. Islam takes sin very seriously and requires punishing sin as Allah commands, whether the sin is a violation of religious, civil, or social life.

Regarding human relationship with God, Islam considers any

form of blasphemy to be the worst of sins. Sharia law suggests various punishments for blasphemy, and in some Islamic countries, that includes death. Regarding human relationships, murder and adultery are sins under Sharia law. The law suggests various punishments for these sins, which, depending on a variety of circumstances, can include death in some Islamic countries.

How the above Aspects of the Muslim Worldview May Affect You

The Islamic country Sheba and Samir came from was run by a dictator with a strict religious government. Before they met and married, they were attending the same university. The university had separate female and male sections, and it was forbidden for males and females to interact.

During lunch breaks, females ate on one side of the university courtyard while males ate on the opposite side. While eating lunch, Samir saw Sheba's face uncovered from across the courtyard. Samir thought Sheba was the most beautiful girl he had ever seen. He was smitten. Except for knowing she was a fellow student in the same university, Samir did not know Sheba's name or anything else about her.

It took weeks of planning and effort, but Samir devised a communication plan where he and Sheba left written notes for each other in secret locations. Eventually, Sheba agreed to meet with Samir in a nearby public park. There Samir sat with a picnic snack on a table facing west, while Sheba sat with her snack on a different table facing the opposite direction. They picked a nonpeak time so they could talk without being heard by anyone else.

Samir began courting Sheba in this way, and eventually she agreed to marry him. Samir's plan then was to go meet Sheba's father and seek his blessing in pursuing his daughter in marriage. But before that happened, the religious police in their country caught them talking one day in the park. They were convicted and sentenced for the forbidden act of unmarried men and women talking to one another. The punishment, multiple lashes by a whip on their backs, was carried out by the religious police, and it left permanent scars. Despite these painful events, their parents gave their blessings, and they were married while in college in their birth country.

Jane and Norm introduced me to Samir and Sheba after they had already been living in America for a few months. We became friends, and Sheba and Samir often went to church with me and joined me in Bible study. On a summer day, they accepted an invitation to go sightseeing with me. By that time, they trusted me enough to share their story with me.

One day I asked how they felt about the differences between living in America compared to their birth country. Samir and Sheba shared thoughts that are common and typical with most Muslims: while they loved many aspects of life in America, they wished the country was godlier and more spiritual. They also shared that they felt they would need to move to a more religious environment, a place that was not as "immoral," when the time came to raise a family.

Since they were reading the Bible, they thought Psalm 84 (NIV) was a good reflection of their perspective on why they felt they needed to move to an Islamic country:

> How lovely is your dwelling place, Lord Almighty! My soul yearns, even faints, for the courts of the Lord; my heart and flesh cry out for the living God … Blessed are those who dwell in your house; they are ever praising you. Blessed are those whose strength is in you, whose hearts are set on pilgrimage … Better is one day in your courts than a thousand elsewhere; I would rather be a doorkeeper in the house of my God than dwell in the tents of the wicked.

Imagine that. Even though Sheba and Samir had lived in an Islamic country ruled by a ruthless dictator and had suffered a penalty for breaking a code in Sharia law, they still longed for an Islamic country. The reason for this is that, like most devout Muslims, they were mindful of the kingdom of God. They view life from a spiritual, eternal perspective rather than an earthly, temporary one. In their worldview, God is going to set up His eternal kingdom, when/where Sharia law will be the law of paradise, with God as king and judge.

To Samir and Sheba, the government in their Islamic birth country is very imperfect and harsh. At the same time, they see it as aiming to be what God desires: a theocracy representing the one true God as model for a wayward world. As imperfect as it was as a human-run country, they believed it still was godlier and a more righteous representation of God's law and desire for all humans. Because of that belief, they viewed Islamic countries as God's vehicles by which humankind would receive the blessing of knowing the one true God.

6 and 7. Blessed or Punished

The sixth and seventh similarities between the Old Testament nation of Israel and the Islamic worldview is that God promised blessings if His people obeyed and punishment if they did not.

The people of the Old Testament nation of Israel saw their wealth and prosperity as unmistakable signs of God's blessing. When God was pleased with them, He subdued their enemies, the non-Jewish nations around them.

Islam expanded rapidly in territory and number of followers after its birth around AD 610. That expansion lasted around one thousand years until the sixteenth century. This is typically viewed by Islam as God's pleasure and favor with what Islam was doing. Muslims believe that God blessed Islam's followers by subduing the non-Islamic nations around them.

Just as God promised blessings for obedience, He also promised punishment for disobedience. Islam's worldview is that God punished the Old Testament nation of Israel for their disobedience to the extent that only a remnant remains after they were defeated by non-Jewish nations around them. God used Gentile nations as His judgment instruments against His nation and people.

Some Muslims believe that God must be displeased with Islam because, ever since the sixteenth century, Islamic nations have typically been defeated by infidel (non-Islamic) nations. The sense is that perhaps God has been using these Christianized nations as His judgment instruments against Islamic nations and people to the extent that He allowed the modern-day nation of Israel to be established in their midst.

Understanding Jihad

The word *jihad* is often used by Western media outlets as they report on any Islamic terrorist activities, including violence related to the Arab/Israeli conflict. The literal meaning of the word jihad is "struggle." Most often, however, in the Arabic or Islamic context, jihad is used to refer to the spiritual struggle against sin.

Have you ever heard about a spiritual war taking place within Christianized nations?

I have heard many Christian leaders and individuals refer to this spiritual war that is making Christianized nations less Christian and more secular and thus less moral. This "war" (or struggle) has many battlegrounds upon which Christians disagree. Some examples include topics such as homosexuality and abortion that spark heated debates.

- What should be done about gay marriage? Should the law of our nation define marriage as only between a man and a woman or as between two individuals regardless of gender?
- When does life begin? Is abortion murder? Should Christians take legal and political actions to reverse court decisions that made abortion legal?

In Islamic terms, these kinds of questions would be a typical usage for the word *jihad* (struggle). And just like there are some major current struggles within Christian circles in Christianized nations, ongoing major struggles (jihads) exist within Islamic circles in Islamic nations. Two interconnected Islamic struggles, or "jihads," are: 1) how to get back into good standings with God and 2) how to establish the kingdom of God on earth.

The jihad is about how Islam can or should achieve these goals.

As you can imagine, there is much disagreement among Islamic theologians, scholars, and leaders about the answers to the above questions. Muslims typically fall into one of two major categories, and the views held by those in each category often shape their answers to these questions.

Extremist Muslims

Some Muslims are "extremists" who have the tendency to become "radical." Islamic terrorists typically come from this extremist category.

Islamic terrorist groups—solo terrorists as well—justify their murderous actions as obedience to Allah. This twisted justification comes from a common misunderstanding of Islam's holy literature. We know this because they often include in their propaganda or statements that they believe their actions are necessary to get back into good standing with Allah and help usher in the kingdom. Their beliefs and convictions are so strong that they are willing to die for them (even by their own hand in suicide attacks).

I mentioned previously that it is estimated that around 10 percent of all Muslims have the propensity to become extremists.[33] But what about the other 90 percent?

---

[33] "The World's Muslims: Religion, Politics and Society," *Pew Research Center,* April 30, 2013, http://www.pewforum.org/2013/04/30/the-worlds-muslims-religion-politics-society-overview/.

The Forgotten Majority

The murderous actions of Islamic terrorists dominate the news on a regular basis, and rightly so. But this focus can also make Christians suspicious and fearful of all Muslims and brand them all as extremists. Hopefully by now you already know that is not true. Around 90 percent of Muslims are not extremists. As Christians, we have been charged with sharing the truth with everyone—including, or perhaps especially, Muslims.

How Does the Muslim Jihad (Struggle) Affect You?

Sheba and Samir, like most Muslims, are anti-extremism. Since they moved to America, there have been numerous Islamic terrorist attacks worldwide. When Jane and Norm got to know Samir and Sheba well, they asked them about their views on such attacks and were relieved by their response. Samir and Sheba shared views that are common among most Muslims: They despise terrorism. They view each murderous attack with horror and disdain.

Samir and Sheba also felt a bit defensive about their culture. They believed that the media in Christianized nations did not portray Muslims completely or accurately because they failed to mention that the majority of Muslims are against terrorism. As a result, Christians were left with the false impression that all Muslims have the propensity to carry out terrorist attacks—something that simply isn't true.

Samir and Sheba later confided that the media in Islamic countries also did not portray Christianized nations or Christians completely or accurately. As a result, that left Muslims with the false impression that Christians, in general, are immoral and that they view Islam and Muslims as their enemies. For example, Samir and Sheba had read in their birth country many Islamic media reports about people who called themselves Christian committing hate crimes (184 in 2014 in

America) against Muslims in Christianized nations.[34] Having lived in America for some time, they now understood that perpetrators of hate crimes did not act on behalf of Christianity. Some of these evildoers may call themselves "Christian," but their actions and hateful beliefs would never be justified by Christianity.

Similarly, Samir and Sheba acknowledged that those who call themselves Muslims and commit terrorist acts and try to justify it in the name of Islam are not true Muslims. They, in fact, believed that these terrorists should be eliminated.

The Widespread Opportunity

By now I hope you have a better understanding of the Muslim worldview. It is also worth noting that the best way to understand the worldview of an individual Muslim is to directly ask the Muslim you know. Muslims, like most people, are typically glad to share their religious beliefs and cultural views that form their own unique worldview under the overall Muslim worldview.

Samir and Sheba were open to the friendship that Jane and Norm offered. They wanted to be understood more accurately by Christians, and they wanted to gain a better understanding of Christians. That openness, which is common, eventually resulted in Sheba and Samir attending church and participating in a Bible study with their Christian friends.

You and I have the opportunity and responsibility to help change the world by being part of the solution with the majority of Muslims who are not extremists. We can follow the examples of those whose stories have been shared in this book. Jane, Norm, Mary, Joe, and so many other ordinary believers are answering God's call to take

---

[34] 2014 Hate Crime Statistics, *FBI:UCR,* Accessed Oct. 16, 2018, https://www.fbi.gov/about-us/cjis/ucr/hate-crime/2014/topic-pages/victims_final; Siemaszko, Corky, "Hate Attacks on Muslims in U.S. Spike After Recent Acts of Terrorism," *NBC News,* Dec. 20, 2015, https://www.nbcnews.com/news/us-news/hate-attacks-muslims-u-s-spike-after-recent-acts-terrorism-n482456.

part in the movement of being ambassadors to Muslims with the gospel. Through their examples of love, generosity, and prayer, we see that Jesus has the power to transform even the most devoted Muslim seeker's heart.

CHAPTER 8

The Second Essential: Person of Peace

Lynn Smith's home Bible study group felt God leading them to expand their outreach and step out of their comfort zones. In response, they decided to do something they had never done before: they went door-to-door, inviting each of their neighbors to their weekly Bible study.

For Lynn, a quiet introvert, the experience felt challenging, awkward, and frustrating. Her spirits dampened as one after another, her neighbors declined the invitation. A rush of relief swept over Lynn when, finally, one named Rose agreed to come to the study.

Everyone in the home group was excited to meet Rose. That next week, they began the meeting by having each member share a brief testimony and a bit about themselves. Then came Rose's turn to introduce herself to the group.

"My name is Rose. I'm Muslim. My father is the imam of the ... " she said, naming the local mosque.

Those simple words, "I'm Muslim," sent Lynn into silent panic. After Rose finished her introduction, Lynn politely announced a break and asked her husband, Dave, to join her in the kitchen to help with the snacks. In fearful, hushed voices, the Smiths discussed what they should do. You see, they did not know *anything* about Islam. They had never met a Muslim before, let alone befriended one who was the daughter of an imam (the equivalent of a pastor). They wondered why Rose had come. Hadn't Lynn made it clear that this was a *Bible* study?

Not knowing what else to do, the Smiths sought God in prayer and asked for His wisdom. The answer was simple: proceed with the Bible study as normal.

Even with that confirmation, concerns continued to surface. What if Rose asked tough questions or tried to convert them to Islam or wanted to debate theology they did not know how to address?

The Smiths already felt ill-equipped to lead a Bible study. Neither of them had seminary training and possessed only basic knowledge of the Bible. They did not consider themselves Bible scholars, something they believed was required to engage a Muslim. Despite their doubts and fears, God's direction to proceed with the Bible study as planned seemed clear. The couple rejoined the group with snacks in hand and in faithful obedience, began the Bible study.

Week after week, Rose returned to the Smiths' home group Bible study. She even brought along her three children. And each week, God increased the home group's confidence and their love for Rose and her family. She accepted a Bible as a gift and surprised the group by regularly completing her Bible study assignments.

As they studied the Bible together, Rose shared what Muslims believed. She explained what Islam and the Quran taught in comparison to the Bible on the different subjects they discussed. For the Smiths' home group members, learning about Islam through a Muslim was a first. During the weekly meetings, they all learned new things and felt a sense of mutual edification.

Secretly, the group began praying for the salvation of Rose and her family. Emboldened by the Holy Spirit, they began praying in Jesus's name with Rose, which she gladly accepted. After around three months, Rose, along with her husband and children, began attending church regularly. One year later, Rose became the first in her family to accept Jesus Christ as Lord and Savior and be baptized. Within another year, Rose's husband accepted Christ and was baptized. Today, he and Rose are raising their young children as Christians.

Rose now spends as much of her time as possible helping the lost find and follow Jesus. Only God knows how many people He will bring into the kingdom through Rose. And it all began with Lynn (an iHOPE workshop alumnus) and her Bible study group committing to doing the second of the five essentials every Christian must know and do when engaging Muslims for Christ.

The Second Essential for Christians to Know and Do: Look for Good Soil

In the previous chapter, we examined the foundational beliefs of Islam. Understanding how these beliefs impact a Muslim person's worldview allows us to see how God's word might be able to take root in the heart of someone who is seeking the truth. Our job, as kingdom builders, is to be on the lookout for people whose hearts (soil) God has prepared to accept the gospel seed.

God created the only seed that can give eternal life, which is the gospel, the good news of Christ as Lord and Savior. For the gospel seed to grow into a fruitful harvest, it needs to be planted into fertile soil, which is a heart God prepared to accept it.

In the story above, Lynn and the Bible study group responded to God in faithful obedience by inviting people to study His word with them. As a result, God led them to Rose, a Muslim whose heart God had prepared to be fertile soil that accepted the gospel seed.

Let us examine a couple of Bible passages that teach us more about this second essential to reach Muslims (or anyone, really) with the gospel.

The Only Way to Jesus

In John 6:44 (NIV) Jesus says, "No one can come to me unless the Father who sent me draws him."

That verse does not imply that *some* can come to faith without first being drawn by God. In fact, it clearly states that *no one* will be receptive to the good news of Jesus Christ unless God the Father first gives her or him the desire or inclination to want to know Christ. In other words, 100 percent of the Muslims who have ever accepted

Christ were first drawn by the Father. That verse also means that Muslims who will be receptive to the gospel seed are those whose hearts God the Father is turning into fertile soil. If we concentrate our efforts on finding those people, the people whom God is already drawing to Himself, our efforts to share the gospel will be more effective and more fruitful.

In the story above, God prepared Rose's heart for Lynn's invitation, and Rose accepted. From my experience and perspective, I can see that the Father has prepared the hearts of countless Muslims for the gospel seed. The harvest is plentiful, but we need more believers like Lynn and her Bible study group to go to find these people of peace and to plant gospel seed in the fertile soil God has prepared.

My encouragement to you is to follow Lynn's example. Step out in prayerful and faithful obedience and invite people to study God's word with you. Even if many reject your invitation like Lynn's neighbors did, our Father will eventually lead you to the person He is drawing to the Son. In this process, you will get to experience the joy and fulfillment of seeing others come to Christ and of watching your eternal family grow.

The Only Way to Accept Jesus

Now let us review a second passage about finding a person whose heart God prepared to accept the gospel seed. In 1 Corinthians 12:3 (NIV), we read, "No one can say 'Jesus is Lord' except in the Holy Spirit."

This verse that does not imply that anyone at any time is able to know the true identity of Jesus as God the Son and accept Him as her or his Lord and Savior; God the Holy Spirit is the one who must reveal that truth.

That means that the only Muslims who will accept Jesus are the ones whom God, through His Holy Spirit, is opening their spiritual eyes to understand that Jesus is the Son of God and softening their hearts to accept Him as their Lord and Savior. In light of this verse, we know 100 percent of the Muslims who have ever accepted Christ did so because the Holy Spirit prepared their hearts to hear and accept the gospel. We can share the gospel with anyone, but when we concentrate our efforts by prayerfully seeking out those whom the Holy Spirit has prepared, we are more likely to be fruitful and multiply with Muslims.

In the story above, it was not Lynn's persuasive reasoning that caused Rose to grasp who Jesus was and accept Him; rather, it was the Holy Spirit who opened Rose's spiritual eyes to recognize the deity of Christ and accept Him as her personal Lord and Savior.

As Christians, we know these two truths: 1) it is the Father who draws lost people to Christ, and 2) it is the Holy Spirit who reveals Christ's deity to them and enables them to accept Him as their Savior. But in this case, knowledge and practice don't always align. I have seen many people grow frustrated with the lack of response to the gospel seeds they are trying to plant because they are either ignorant (or forgetful) of these truths, or they simply ignore the fact that it is God who does the work in people's hearts and believe they can convince people to follow Jesus. The following scenarios illustrate the vital distinctions and outreach practices of the LEM (least effective majority) and the MEM (most effective minority) we discussed in chapter 1 and how the heart of the hearer makes all the difference in the results.

Extremely Qualified Sam

Sam is a sincere and well-meaning Christian who has engaged Muslims with Christianity for about twenty-five years. Sam has traveled extensively to many Islamic countries worldwide. He is an expert on Islam and their holy books, including the Quran. Sam is also an expert on the peoples of the various Islamic regions and their politics and cultures.

Sam is very well educated and holds multiple college degrees, including a master of theology and master of Islamic studies.

Least Fruitful Approach

Sam used his extensive education, knowledge, relevant background, and high intelligence to engage Muslims worldwide on six continents. Sam and Muslims loved reasoning with each other about Christianity and Islam, and even the most devout Muslims often walked away from their conversations with Sam feeling as if he had better reasoning for Christianity than they did for Islam.

Sam's approach requires a tremendous amount of knowledge and preparation that are extremely difficult to duplicate, resulting in the fewest number of workers in God's harvest field.

Least Fruitful Soil

Sam knew intellectually that it is the Father who draws the lost to Jesus. But in practice, Sam took his own approach and depended on his own appeal (charm, charisma, etc.) and efforts to draw Muslims to Christ. Sam also knew intellectually that it is the Holy Spirit who enables people to accept Christ, but in practice, Sam used his education and reasoning skills to try to plant seeds in hardened soil.

Sam did not bother to try to find and connect with Muslims whose hearts God had prepared for the gospel seed. As a result, Sam invested his time and efforts with Muslims whose hearts were still too hard to receive the gospel seed.

Least Fruitful Cycle

Sam, as is typical with the LEM, persisted with his efforts to soften hardened Muslim hearts, which, as we have discussed in this chapter, only God can do. For around twenty-five years, Sam was distracted in a frustrating cycle of planting in hardened soil that rejected the gospel seed.

Least Fruit

Despite all of Sam's educational and experienced qualifications as an elite missionary (EM), in twenty-five years of engaging Muslims, he proudly shared with me multiple times that he had led eight Muslims to Jesus as Lord and Savior.

Less-Qualified Renod

Before founding iHOPE Ministries, I attended some of Sam's lectures on the topic of engaging Muslims with Christ. Sam even took time to personally teach me some of the methods and techniques that he used to engage Muslims. I also watched him engage Muslims. As I listened to and observed Sam, I was in awe of his knowledge and skills—knowledge and skills that I lacked. Overwhelmed by the reality that I couldn't duplicate Sam's approach, I concluded that I would need extensive training to reach Muslims with the gospel of Jesus Christ. Even with that training, I knew that it was unlikely that any Muslims would believe in Jesus because of my efforts. After all, I reasoned to myself, if Sam, with all his EM qualifications and twenty-five-year track record, helped bring eight Muslims to faith in Jesus as Lord and Savior, then I should be overjoyed if even one believed.

Despite all my fears and hesitations, I responded to God by reaching out to Muslims. At the time, unlike Sam, I had only basic knowledge of Islam, their holy books, and some of their cultures. Unlike Sam, I am still a novice regarding the politics of the regions and the variety of the people groups of Islam. Unlike Sam, I did not attend college, nor did I have any professional theological training.

More Fruitful Approach

Despite my lack of academic qualifications and my sinful past, God used me to plant gospel seeds in the hearts of more than two thousand Muslims in my first five years of ministry. Because I didn't have extensive education and training, I focused on what I knew I could do. Using simple efforts, which comprise the same five essentials that I am sharing with you in this book, I saw more than sixty Muslims quickly accept Christ as their Lord and Savior. Through ongoing efforts of other believers who have partnered with me in using the five essentials, more than one thousand of the two thousand have accepted Jesus as of the writing of this book.

God saved one thousand Muslim souls in five years through me and our MEM partners compared to eight through Sam and his LEM methods in twenty-five years. Why is that?

The First Secret to Success

I believe that, through the process of finding fertile soil for the gospel seed, God wants us to learn three important lessons. The first is that our dependence must be upon God—not ourselves. God has been teaching humanity this lesson since time began. It's why He gave Adam and Eve the choice between total dependence on Him or reliance on self. Part of what characterized paradise before humans sinned was total dependence on God, and it will be the same after the second coming when humans are restored to paradise. Dependence on God keeps us close to Him.

Regarding the work of transforming the Muslim world for Christ, God teaches us that if we want heavenly results, we must depend on Him completely. That means we must depend on God to lead us to the Muslims whose hearts He has prepared to receive the gospel seed.

Sam's actions appeared to show his dependence on his knowledge, skills, and methods to produce outreach success with Muslims. After twenty-five years, eight Muslims became believers in Christ. In comparison, I could not and did not depend on Sam's elaborate methods because of my limited knowledge and skills. Instead, I depended on God to take me to the Muslims He was drawing to Himself and whose hearts He was preparing to accept the gospel seed.

Dependence on God gives us more faith and courage to obey God.

We can then take a confident step toward what appears impossible, like Israel crossing the Red Sea. God is eager to have you accomplish in Him what appears to be impossible, such as transforming the Muslim world for Christ.

The Second Secret to Success

The second lesson we learn in this process of depending on God for success in reaching Muslims with the gospel is to trust Him with everything, including the results.

Adam and Eve sinned when they did not trust God adequately. They bought into the lie that Satan was selling and decided to partake of the tree of the knowledge of good and evil. Since then, humans have suffered needlessly and labor continually. Suffering and toiling are the opposite of what God made available in the garden of Eden and of what we will have when we are restored to paradise.

Sam's actions appeared to show his trust in a method and his own knowledge and skills to produce fruit with Muslims. The result was stressful, frustrating labor that resulted in a small amount of fruit; meanwhile, unable to master those complicated methods, I had to trust the Lord of the harvest to produce fruit through me. God wants to produce an abundant harvest with Muslims through you and will do so when you trust Him rather than your own efforts and expertise.

The Third Secret to Success

The third lesson God teaches us as we depend on and trust Him for results is that we must humble ourselves before Him. As we seek fertile soil for the gospel seed, we must humbly recognize that neither we nor any specific methods will produce the harvest He desires. If people were saved by our efforts, expertise, or methods, we would get the glory instead of God. Humility keeps us working to do things God's way, not ours, for His glory, not ours. Humility helps keep us dependent on God, trusting Him for the result as we faithfully move forward.

Biblical Illustrations of These Success Secrets

In the Bible, God repeatedly teaches us these lessons on success. Here are just a few of the many ways God gave His people victory:

- In Joshua 6, God gave His people the victory over Jericho when priests joined the army, blew trumpets, and marched around the fortified wall of the city.
- In Joshua 8, God gave the Israelites victory through vastly different battle tactics and thirty thousand men (no priests this time).
- In Judges 7, when God's people were outnumbered 135,000 to 32,000, God won the battle in an unusual way. This time God reduced their numbers to 300, so they were outnumbered 450 to 1. God gave them the victory this time while they blew trumpets and smashed clay jars that had torches in them.
- In 2 Chronicles 20, God gave His people another seemingly impossible victory as they sang and praised God.

Whether military victories, personal successes, or miracles, God never did the same thing twice. God gave His people success, each time in a different way and with varying details. Why is that?

I believe the answer to that question is easily found within the context of the Bible: God does not want us to look for a method or a formula because then we could become arrogant as we depended on and trusted in a method or a formula. That self-reliance and pride are the essence of living in a fallen and sinful world.

Instead, God wants us to rely on Him. He wants us to learn and practice the principles that existed in paradise before humankind sinned and will exist when paradise is restored: be humble before our loving God, depend on Him to provide success, and trust and obey His ongoing guidance.

These three lessons are vital for us to learn if we want to be fruitful and multiply with Muslims. We know they are essential because Jesus taught them to His followers in Luke 10 when He revealed the importance of finding what the MEM refers to as the "person of peace." That is a person whose heart is ready to hear the gospel.

Find Good Soil

How can we determine if a Muslim is the one whom God is drawing to Jesus? The truth is, we can't know for sure. Finding a Muslim (or any non-Christian) whose heart is good soil for the gospel seed is an art, not a science or math equation. The only way to become good in an art or a sport is through practice. That said, there are ways we can increase the possibility to know whether God is drawing a specific Muslim to Christ. I will cover some of these in the next two chapters, but for now, let's begin by reviewing Jesus's teaching in Luke 10:5–7. These verses helped me as I worked to learn the art of planting gospel seeds with Muslims whose hearts are good soil.

> Whenever you enter someone's home, first say, "May God's peace be on this house." If those who live there are peaceful, the blessing will stand, if they are not, the blessing will return to you. Don't move around from home to home. Stay in one place. (Luke 10:5–7 NLT)

The following are some of the insights I have applied from the passage:

1. **Focus on one clear, God-dependent message**. Verse 5 states, "Whenever you enter someone's home, first say, 'May God's peace be on this house.'" To identify whether a Muslim

may have a desire (God the Father drawing them) to talk about the good news of Jesus, I need to have a clear initial Christ-centered message. Then the Muslim can decide whether he or she wants to proceed with me regarding the Jesus-centered subject.

2. **Make a quick determination**. Verse 6 states, "If those who live there are peaceful, the blessing will stand, if they are not, the blessing will return to you." If a Muslim decides to proceed with the Jesus-centered subject, then he or she may be one whose heart God is preparing to receive a gospel seed. If the Muslim declines to proceed, then God has not yet chosen to prepare this person's heart for the gospel seed.
3. **Focus on the person of peace**. Verse 7 begins with, "Don't move around from home to home. Stay in one place. " If a Muslim decides to proceed with the Jesus-centered encounter, then I am to follow through with the relationship to plant the gospel seed in fertile soil (heart) and take care of it to maximize a fruitful harvest. The person in this passage (and in Matthew 10:5–15) is typically referred to as the person of peace. Within the context of this book, a person of peace is one whose heart is good soil because God has prepared her or his heart for the gospel seed. The person of peace is one whom the Father is drawing to Jesus, and the Holy Spirit is preparing them to know Christ as Lord and Savior.

The process of successfully connecting with a person of peace requires us to be humble and dependent on God and to trust Him through it all. It is God who leads us to the right person, at the right time, with His message. It is God who puts it all together to produce the fruitful harvest. It is very fulfilling and exciting to be instruments like that in the hands of the one and only Redeemer.

The following are stories to demonstrate how I applied this essential practice to planting gospel seeds into the hearts of two thousand Muslims within five years, resulting in a fruitful harvest of around one thousand souls. (Side note: These one thousand Christians, all with Muslim backgrounds, were discipled to become fruitful and multiply, which creates an exponentially reproducing harvest.)

Finding a Person of Peace Quickly

Sometimes after workshops, we send out attendees like Jesus did in Luke 10:1, two by two, to put what they've just learned into practice. We go around apartment communities where Muslim refugees live (Syrians, for example), near Islamic mosques, to Islamic stores (clothing, books, gifts, etc.), and to restaurants where we are likely to encounter Muslims.

One fruitful *clear, God-dependent message* that some of our teams have shared with Muslims is, "I am a Christian. I am offering God's word, the Bible, as a gift. Would you like one?" We offer the Bible in print in multiple languages as well as in eBooks, audiobooks, and a downloadable app on smart devices that is available in thousands of languages.

After one event, I was teamed with Clay, who works as a musician, and we went to apartment communities where Muslim refugees lived. As we walked through the complex, we introduced ourselves with the one clear, God-dependent message statement mentioned above. Most Muslims did not accept the Bible gift from us. We made a *quick determination* that none of these Muslims were yet the person of peace God wanted us to find. Their rejection meant that the blessing returned to us and that we ought to keep looking for the person in whom God was already working.

A few Muslims did not accept the Bible gift, but they did want to talk with us. They proceeded to tell us that the Bible was corrupted and that we should read a Quran. They were eager to evangelize us into Islam and would only respond to us with argumentative statements. They were willing to debate Christianity as compared to Islam, but we were not there to debate. Again, we made the quick determination that none of these Muslims were yet the person of peace for whom we were seeking. Interestingly, these are the types of Muslims on whom those in the LEM end up focusing. These Muslims are willing to engage in conversation, but their hearts are not yet ready to receive the gospel message.

A few Muslims did accept the Bible gift from us. When a Muslim received our *one clear God-dependent message,* our blessing stood. We were then able to make a *quick determination* to *focus* on this Muslim as the potential *person of peace* God wanted us to find. These are the types of Muslim the MEM focus on.

When we found a Muslim who accepted our gift, we stopped and visited with that possible person of peace. Barakat was such a Muslim. Barakat saw us talking with other Muslims, and he was curious about who we were and what we were doing. When he approached us, we told him we were Christians and that we were offering God's word, the Bible. With this clear, God-dependent message, we offered him a Bible. Barakat accepted a printed Arabic/English Bible with enthusiasm and immediately began reading it. Right away, he had questions, and we began an impromptu Bible study.

Barakat did not make any argumentative statements, nor did he desire comparative religion debates; rather, Barakat had a tremendous thirst and hunger to continue reading the Bible. The more he read, the more questions he had, which led to ongoing Bible studies individually with Clay, me, and another mature Christian we later introduced to Barakat. All that led to Barakat attending church, where he eventually accepted Jesus as Lord and Savior and was baptized.

Prayer: An Easy Way to a Person of Peace

Another fruitful, clear, God-dependent message we share with Muslims is to offer to pray for them. Prayer is often met with less resistance than the offer of a Bible. We approach a Muslim with a warm smile and say, "I am a Christian. God put His love for Muslims in my heart. I would love to pray for you. May I?"

It is our experience that only a tiny minority of Muslims respond to our question in an unfriendly manner. When they do, we make a quick determination that this Muslim is not yet a person of peace, and we move on to the next Muslim to whom we feel God may be leading us.

Typically, our question leads to a puzzled look by the Muslim. Some do not even respond to the question; they simply ignore us and keep going. Many Muslims, however, begin a friendly conversation with us. Typically the short conversation ends with many Muslims accepting our offer for us to pray with them.

At that point, we make the following statement and then question: "Since I am a Christian, I ask Jesus to pray on your behalf. If God is willing to do a miracle for you, what would you request of Him?" I then proceed to pray for them, closing the prayer with, "In Jesus's name, amen."

Muslim Woman of Peace

The following story demonstrates how you can maximize your fruitfulness by focusing your efforts on a person of peace and minimize your time with those whose hearts are still hardened toward the gospel.

I was having lunch with a small group of iHOPE workshop alumni at a restaurant owned by a Muslim couple. The owners are warm, friendly, and hospitable, the food is delicious, and best of all, Muslims frequent the restaurant. At one point, I said to the owners, "We are Christians. God put His love for Muslims in each of our hearts. We would love to pray for you. May we?"

The couple gently responded with, "Thank you for asking. Although we appreciate your offer, we will pass at this time. Jesus was a great prophet, but we do not believe he was the Son of God." Then the husband went on to share with us his view that God's progressive revelation to humankind culminated with the Quran through Muhammad, the last and final prophet. He was willing to talk (debate) with us, comparing Islam with Christianity, but because they rejected our one clear message (prayer for them), we quickly determined they were not yet the persons of peace God wanted us to engage.

Meanwhile, a Muslim woman sat in the restaurant by herself. She looked sad and troubled. Between serving customers, the restaurant owners sat with the woman, Diana, and engaged in a hushed conversation. After watching her for a bit, my wife and I approached her.

I said, "We are with the small group (pointed to our table) over there. We are Christians. God put His love for Muslims in our hearts. You seem troubled or sad about something. We would love to pray for you. May we?"

Diana replied, "Yes, please!"

Then I said, "As Christians, we pray in the name of Jesus and ask Him to pray on your behalf. If God is willing to do a miracle for you, what would you request of Him?"

Diana replied, "I have an older brother. Our parents recently died and left everything to him. My brother has been beating me since then and demanding I move out of the house before his upcoming wedding so he and his wife can live there alone. He is not allowing me to have any of the money our parents left us, and I am not yet equipped to live on my own. Please pray that my brother will stop beating me and that he will allow me to have a share of the inheritance."

So the small team lovingly circled around Diana, and we prayed for her, ending our prayers with "in Jesus's name, amen." I wasn't sure I would ever see Diana again, so I wanted to model to the group how to plant a quick gospel seed with a Muslim. I said, "We believe what God tells us in the Bible, Romans 10:9 (NIV), 'If you confess with your mouth that Jesus is Lord and believe in your heart that God raised him from the dead, you will be saved.' Diana, do you believe that?"

Diana quickly rejected Jesus as Lord and Savior or as anything more than a prophet. She did, however, accept a church invitation from a member of the group and later attended. She then accepted a Bible as a gift and did Bible studies.

Four months after that initial encounter, my wife and I thought about Diana and wondered how she was, so we called her. It was the first time my wife and I had spoken with her since the day we had first met.

Diana exclaimed, "God answered your prayers!"

Karen and I were not sure which prayer Diana was referring to, so I asked, "Which prayer?"

Diana shared that since the day we prayed with her in the name of Jesus at the restaurant, her brother had not beaten her. He had also given Diana her share of the inherited money, and he was no longer trying to evict her out of the house they had inherited. My wife and I thought we ought to seize the momentum, so we asked Diana about a new prayer request that we could pray in the name of Jesus.

Without hesitation, Diana said, "Pray that God will reveal to me the truth about whether Jesus is a prophet or the Son of God and that God will soften my hardened heart to accept and respond to that truth."

Diana's story is ongoing as she seeks God's truth. Her story and Barakat's illustrate how we can quickly find persons of peace. Planting seeds in hearts God has prepared for the gospel is essential to having a fruitful harvest. This minimizes frustrations and maximizes results.

Finding a Person of Peace Where the Gospel Is Illegal

I often get asked about how to find a person of peace and plant gospel seeds in nations where it is dangerous or illegal to do so. The following story demonstrates the answers.

Dave, a missionary, leads a small group of Christians who are in Islamic countries where it is dangerous and/or illegal to share the gospel or try to convert a Muslim to Christianity. Yet they willingly risk their lives to expand God's kingdom.

In just four years, their efforts have resulted with dozens of house churches led now by more than fifty Christians from Muslim backgrounds. These former Muslims accepted Christ through the work of Dave and his team, and they have been discipled to be fruitful and multiply with other Muslims in the region. Through their continued sharing of the gospel, more than one thousand Muslims risk their lives weekly to attend worship gatherings and Bible studies at these house churches to learn the truth about Jesus.

Dave seeks persons of peace by saying something like this: "My name is Dave. I am a Christian. God put His love for Muslims in my heart. I feel like God is leading me to pray for you, and I do so in the name of Jesus. May I pray for you?" That typically leads to a friendly conversation with the Muslim who agrees to have Dave pray for him.

Dave then is purposeful in creating an opportunity to share a quick summary of his testimony, which sounds a bit like this: "I used to be full of anger and hate toward Muslims. But after I accepted Jesus as my Savior, He took away my anger and hate and replaced it with forgiveness and love. Now I follow God's teachings in the Bible and share His love with Muslims, even where it seems I am risking my life to do so."

Even where it is illegal to share the gospel, it is legal to pray for a Muslim, even in the name of Jesus, and to share your testimony. I call Dave's legal approach "The Art of Sharing the Gospel Legally Even Where It Is Illegal to Do So." More importantly, this approach follows the teachings of the Bible that we studied so far in this chapter.

As a result, Dave and his teams end up with Muslims who are persons of peace, eventually planting seeds into hearts God has prepared for the gospel. They do so in ways that minimize personal risks and frustrations and within four years have produced plentiful fruit.

Dave and these small teams are living out the book of Acts. In Acts we read many stories where there was social and legal opposition to the proclamation of the gospel. There was also persecution, even unto death. Even in those dire circumstances and despite opposition, we see the faithful obedience of the followers of Jesus.

Dreams and Visions

One of the ways God prepares a Muslim's heart for the gospel seed is through dreams and visions. I am sharing the following with you as a side note in this chapter about finding good soil because I do not want you to be completely surprised if this ever happens to you.

Various books and sources have reported that hundreds of thousands of Muslims have had visions and dreams about Christ, or about someone coming to tell them about Christ. A few years ago, I experienced this for the first time when a Muslim woman, whom we did not know, approached my wife and me and told us that she saw me in a vivid dream. She was told in the dream that I would have a message for her from God.

Caught off guard, I stood there speechless. Finally, I blurted out, "God wants you to know that 'if you declare with your mouth, "Jesus is Lord," and believe in your heart that God raised him from the dead, you will be saved ... For the Scriptures says, everyone who believes in him will not be put to shame' (Romans 10:9–11 ESV). Will you accept Jesus as your saving gift from God?"

The Muslim woman did not accept Jesus that day, but she allowed me to pray for her in the name of Jesus. She also accepted a Bible as a gift and later joined us for Bible study. I then connected her with Christians in her area. Since then, she has had ongoing Bible studies with them and attends a home church group.

I have a few Christian friends who have also had Muslims approach them about dreams and visions they've had. This has occurred in Christianized countries where the gospel is legal and in Islamic countries where it is not. So many times, we've seen these divine appointments and encounters result with Muslims accepting Christ as Lord and Savior.

God may lead you to a Muslim person of peace who tells you about a vision or a dream they had. You do not need to worry about what to say if that happens to you. Like He did with me, the Holy Spirit will put the words in your mouth in that moment.

Fun Ways to Find Person of Peace

Here are a few more fun ways that iHOPE workshop alumni have used to find a Muslim person of peace. These approaches may spark additional ideas that fit with your God-given gifts or personality.

Cultures and Meals

Chris, a bank employee, approaches Muslims in his Christianized nation with a loving smile and a curious question: "Hi, I'm Chris. I am a Christian. I love learning about different cultures and especially their food. Where are you originally from?"

Chris has also traveled to Islamic countries, on his own and with iHOPE Ministries, and has used the same approach to meet Muslims there, adjusting his opening statement to "Hi, I'm Chris. I am a Christian from (name of country). God put His love in my heart for your country and people. I would love to learn more about your culture and especially your foods. What is a meal you recommend I try, and where is there a good restaurant that serves it?"

Chris told me that finding the courage to start the conversation can be challenging at first, but the rest is easy. In general, Muslims are friendly and hospitable, and they typically respond enthusiastically to Chris's questions. At some point in the initial conversation, Chris offers to pray for the person in the name of Jesus and/or offers them a Bible.

Chris's interest in culture and love for ethnically diverse foods have resulted in him sharing the love of Christ with many Muslims while learning about their cultures over a meal. Some of them end up being people of peace and accept the prayer and/or the Bible. Using this simple process, both locally and globally, Chris has brought dozens of Muslims to church, engaged in ongoing Bible studies with some of them, and personally led nine Muslims to Christ as Lord and Savior in just a few short years. These new Christians have been or are being discipled to do the same.

Cooking

Beth, who works as an administrative assistant, goes to ethnic grocery stores in her Christianized nation and looks for opportunities to interact with Muslim women. With a warm smile, she initiates conversation by saying, “Hi, I’m Beth. I love to cook, and I want to learn to cook delicious ethnic meals. I’m hoping to find recipes and ingredients in this store. Are there any recipe books or online recipes you recommend?”

Like Chris, Beth has traveled internationally and has used the same approach to meet Muslims. In the past five years, Beth has established friendships with more than ten Muslim women of peace and their families. They teach each other to cook delicious meals and have dinner parties (and outdoor picnics) together with their families. Beth has also dined at the homes of newfound Muslim friends overseas. These contacts have resulted in several long-distance relationships, and she connects regularly with these friends via video calls on computers and smartphones, as well as through social media.

Sports

Roger, a physical education teacher, loves sports. He approaches Muslims in his Christianized nation with a friendly smile and a question: “Hi, I’m Roger. I love sports. I am skilled at several and teach others to improve their skills. But I need lots of help with soccer. Do you play soccer?”

Roger has also traveled internationally to Islamic countries, including with iHOPE Ministries. He has used the same approach to meet Muslims there. In the past five years, Roger has developed dozens of friendships with Muslim persons of peace. He has taught his new friends how to play baseball, football, and basketball and has ongoing games with them. They have done the same with Roger, but with soccer.

Roger, his wife, and their three children are busy and active, maintaining dozens of friendships with Muslims locally and globally. They have given them Bibles, studied the Bible with them, and prayed with them, using social media and video calls with their friends who live in other countries. They have led dozens of Muslims to Jesus as their Lord and Savior, and these new Christians are then discipled to do the same.

Henna

Henna is a temporary tattoo that is typically applied by Muslim women on their hands and feet. They have many variations of types and designs from Islamic countries throughout the world. Muslim women often get together for fun henna parties.

Cathy, a college student, approaches Muslims in her Christianized nation with a warm smile and a fun question: “Hi, I’m Cathy. I am a Christian. I see henna on Muslim women, and some of it is so beautiful. Do you know where to get henna and how to apply such beautiful designs?”

Like Chris, Beth, and Roger, Cathy uses her unique approach to meet Muslims when she travels internationally. In the past five years, Cathy has also formed dozens of friendships with Muslim women and their families. Cathy has had plenty of fun at dozens of henna parties locally and globally and even hosted her own. Cathy prays and studies the Bible with many of these women and has led more than ten Muslims to Christ as their Lord and Savior.

Conversation Partner

When Muslim international students, refugees, and immigrants come to Christianized nations, one of their biggest needs is a language conversation partner. This is simply someone who talks with them in the local language. Refugee settlement agencies and student organizations in the local educational institutions seek volunteers to join them during regularly hosted conversation hours. You are highly likely to meet Muslims at such gatherings.

Trying to explain the meaning of words, phrases, and especially idioms can be fun—even hilarious. Think of common English phrases that could be erroneously interpreted by a non-English speaker:

- At the drop of a hat
- Barking up the wrong tree
- Beating around the bush
- Costs an arm and a leg
- Don't cry over spilled milk
- Cut the mustard
- Heard it on the grapevine
- Hit the sack
- Jump on the bandwagon
- Let the cat out of the bag
- Method to my madness
- Not playing with a full deck
- On the fence
- Heard it straight from the horse's mouth

Jason, a college student, has built friendships with dozens of Muslim persons of peace, and they all began through his volunteer work as a language conversation partner. When traveling to Islamic countries, Jason enjoys working with Muslims who are teaching him their language while he teaches them his language. These international relationships and conversations are continued via video calls and social media and have led to him praying and studying the Bible with many Muslims. Jason has led more than ten Muslims to Jesus as their Lord and Savior who have been or are being discipled to do the same.

Shopping

Cheryl, works in cosmetics, was born and raised in a Christianized nation and had never talked with a Muslim. She wanted to, but she was always afraid to take that first step and initiate conversation. She heard from a friend about iHOPE workshops, so she attended several sessions. As part of inspiring and empowering Christians to help Muslims find and follow Jesus, we periodically take small groups to a local mosque.

Cheryl was scheduled to attend one of our mosque educational events and came to me to inquire where she could purchase a hijab, the veil that Muslim women wear to cover their hair/head and chest. Just as she was asking me, two Muslim women in hijabs walked in our direction. With my encouragement, Cheryl mustered enough courage to overcome her fear and put some of her training into action.

Cheryl walked up to the two Muslim ladies and said, "My name is Cheryl. I am a Christian. I am registered with a Christian group to visit a mosque as part of an educational event. I want to dress respectfully when I go to the mosque. Would you tell me what type of clothes I can wear to cover all my skin, and where can I buy them from? Also, would you teach me how to put on a hijab?"

The Muslim women happily agreed. One of the two turned out to be a person of peace. Since then, she has had ongoing Bible studies with Cheryl and has attended church. Emboldened by that first encounter with a Muslim five years ago, Cheryl has used shopping for clothes as a fun way to connect with Muslim women and find other persons of peace.

What's Your Approach?

The above examples are just a few fun ways to find persons of peace, plant gospel seeds, and be fruitful and multiply as God designed. What is important to remember is that Muslims are often like you: interested in things you are interested in and looking for friends, and while they may be curious about you as a Christian, they may not be bold enough to initiate the conversation. I encourage you to find ways to reach out and befriend Muslims, letting them know from the onset that you are a Christian. Your approach can be as unique and creative as those I've shared from others in this chapter. We would love to hear your stories! Please share them with us by sending us an email at info@iHopeministries.org. Your story may help others discover creative ways that are suitable for them so they can be part of the movement to change the world by sharing Jesus with Muslims.

Don't Wait!

We must remain focused on the main purposes God has for His people: to be fruitful and multiply. This requires that we plant gospel seeds with the persons of peace God has prepared for you.

Some people are hesitant to share the gospel. They will develop long-term friendships with Muslims without ever talking about their faith in Jesus Christ as Lord and Savior or ever having a gospel-centered conversation. One pastor, missionary, and theology professor explained his approach to me this way: "I don't push the gospel unless they are ready for it. I maintain the relationship and wait."

I have seen well-meaning Christians maintain relationships with Muslims for years without ever sharing the gospel because they did not think the Muslim was ready.

We want to be part of the most effective group and focus on planting gospel seeds with Muslims who are already persons of peace instead of being distracted and settling for mere relationships with Muslims who are willing to engage us with anything other than a Christ-centered message. You and I can help change the world by stepping out in faithful obedience and doing our parts in the areas God gifted us to plant gospel seeds, one Muslim person of peace at a time.

CHAPTER 9
The Third Essential: The Bible

Samira and Rahila are Christian women from Muslim backgrounds. They were born and raised in Islamic countries and later moved to a Christianized nation, where they became Christians. Mahmoud is another Christian from a Muslim background. He, too, was born and raised in Islamic countries, but he converted to Christianity there and chose to stay there. All three are now married and raising their children as Christians.

Before they became Christians, they were devout Muslims who studied the Quran and the Hadith and Sunna extensively. They also were very well trained in Islamic apologetics, the reasoned justifications of Islam and its doctrines. Rahila even worked actively to convert Christians into Islam.

After becoming followers of Jesus, they studied the Bible and Christian apologetics. Their testimonies included relevant stories from their extensive Islamic knowledge—which were shared with the hope of leading Muslims to Jesus. Churches, their spouses, and individual Christians supported them financially so they could share the gospel with Muslims in both Christianized and Islamic nations.

Their testimonies included their questions about Islam when they were Muslims and the unsatisfactory answers the Quran offered for these concerns. Samira and Rahila, for example, were troubled by some of the unfavorable references about women in the Quran, Hadith, and Sunna, such as those that follow:

> Men stand superior to women in that God hath preferred some of them over others ... But those (*women*) whose perverseness ye fear, admonish them and remove them into bed-chambers and beat them; but if they submit to you, then do not seek a way against them.
>
> —Quran 4.34 (*The Quran Dilemma,* volume 1)

> I was shown the hell-fire and that the majority of its dwellers were women who were ungrateful ... They are ungrateful to their husbands and are ungrateful for the favors and the good done to them.
>
> —Hadith, Al-Bukhari 1.28

Mahmoud's testimony included questions regarding the teachings of the Quran, Hadith, and Sunna regarding violence, a subject within Islam that troubled him. Mahmoud studied more than one hundred verses from the Quran (like the one below) that call Muslims to war against non-Muslims for the sake of the rule of Islam and as a means of converting people to Islam. He examined related verses in the Hadith and Sunna texts on these subjects and reviewed the various conflicting opinions Islamic commentators and apologists offer on such passages and subjects.

> Kill them wherever ye find them, and drive them out from whence they drive you out; for sedition is worse than slaughter ... Then kill them, for such is the recompense of those that misbelieve ... But fight them that there be no sedition and that the religion may be God's; but if they desist, then let there be no hostility save against the unjust.
>
> —Quran 2.191–193 (*The Quran Dilemma,* volume 1)

Each time Samira, Rahila, or Mahmoud shared their testimonies, they began with Islamic things that troubled them personally, hoping to strike similar sentiments with the Muslim hearer. From there they talked about how they were led to the Bible, Jesus, and Christianity, where they found satisfying answers. Then they would share how a relationship with Christ changed each of their lives, hoping they could help lead Muslims to Jesus as Lord and Savior. Their sincere wish was to inspire similar journeys with the Muslim hearer.

Sincere but Misfocused Methodologies

Samira, Rahila, and Mahmoud combined their extensive Islamic knowledge with their excellent Christian apologetics reasoning skills, hoping to lead Muslims to Jesus as Lord and Savior. The following five examples they used are commonly used by Christians in the LEM who engage Muslims with the gospel.

1. They referred to the common misunderstanding among Muslims that the Trinity means that Christians worship three gods. They explained that Christianity believes in one God, but that He is a triune God. They tried to explain the Trinity using various illustrations, such as the chemical formula of H_2O as one chemical in three forms (water, ice, and steam) or a triangle, which has three sides but is one shape.
2. They used illustrations and parables to explain the need for Jesus as the Son of God to die on the cross as payment for our sins and how His death makes salvation possible for us. For example, they referred to God the Father as the supreme judge and humans as indebted sinners incapable of making the required payment to save themselves. But Jesus, the Son of God, is the only one with enough resources to pay our debt and make full restitution. Jesus now offers Himself as our advocate to pay our debt. If we accept His free gift, then God the Judge accepts it from the Son, and we are saved.

3. To attract Muslims to Jesus and make a case for His deity, they lifted up Jesus's character and deeds as significantly better and holier than those of Muhammad, Islam's prophet.
4. One method they used to lift up Christ is to refer to one passage of the twenty-five in the Quran that refer to Jesus. Quran 3.42–55 mentions the virgin birth, miraculous powers of Christ, and God's special blessings on Jesus's followers. The goal of this method is to lift up Jesus through the Quran to attract Muslims to learn more about Him in the Bible.
5. Knowing that Muslims believe the Bible has been corrupted, they used their wealth of knowledge to answer the objections Muslims have about the Bible. They used sound apologetics to defend the Bible as the true word of God and referred Muslims to the overwhelming evidence, including tens of thousands of manuscripts and books that attest to the authenticity and reliability of the Bible. They believed that this kind of in-depth study and explanation was necessary to convince a Muslim to accept the Bible.

Their Fruit

With zeal for the Lord, Samira, Rahila, and Mahmoud worked tirelessly for several years sharing their testimonies and using their reasoning methodologies to lead Muslims to Christ.

A few Muslims attempted unsuccessfully to persuade them back to Islam; a few Muslims in Islamic nations even issued death sentences for them. Some Muslims wanted to debate with them, but even the most brilliant Muslim debaters often walked away feeling that Samira, Rahila, and Mahmoud had better apologetics reasoning for Christianity than they did for Islam. But most of the Muslims they tried to talk with refused to engage with them.

After several years of planting gospel seeds through their testimonies and reasoning methodologies worldwide, only a handful of Muslims had accepted Bibles or Christ because of their efforts.

Despite the unique advantages they seemed to have—the inside knowledge of Islam, Muslims, similar cultures, strong testimonies as former Muslims, and their brilliant reasoning skills—they did not have a fruitful harvest.

Their Cycle

Even though they had little fruit to show, their unique knowledge and backgrounds made them popular speakers for meetings designed to train Christians to reach out to Muslims. Most of the attendees at those events, including Christians from Muslim backgrounds, could not see themselves doing what Samira, Rahila, and Mahmoud were training them to do.

Very few of them could incorporate the kinds of stories and personal experiences these three had woven into their testimonies. Those who didn't have Muslim backgrounds left those meetings believing that they would need years of study to gain the knowledge Samira, Rahila, and Mahmoud possessed as former Muslims who were well educated on Islam itself. Even if they invested years to gain the knowledge, these approaches also required extensive persuasion, communication, and language skills.

The approaches and methodologies Samira, Rahila, and Mahmoud taught are typical of the LEM; they are intricate and difficult to duplicate. So even after attending their training sessions, the Christians in attendance felt more fearful than inspired about getting involved in helping Muslims find and follow Jesus. Those Christians who did put in the time and effort to master the arguments produced very little fruit. With sincere hearts, they devoted time, energy, and focus to things that weren't effective for bringing Muslims to Christ. Their motives were good, but they had become part of the LEM—the least effective majority.

We will now pause from the story of Samira, Rahila, and Mahmoud and their least fruitful methodologies so we can review a story that reveals the greatest seed ever, guaranteed by God. Seeing the contrast between their story and the one that follows will help explain why some planting approaches are more effective than others. When you understand the difference in these approaches, you can focus your efforts on planting the greatest seed ever in a way that maximizes your fruitfulness.

A Muslim Seeking to Convert Christians

Jalal was a devout Muslim born and raised in the Middle East/North Africa. Like Samira, Rahila, and Mahmoud, Jalal was well educated about Islam and well trained in Islamic apologetics. As an adult, Jalal immigrated to a Christianized nation with the intention of spreading Islam.

Jalal found it difficult to find Christians who would engage him in spiritual conversations. The few Christians who did, including some from Muslim backgrounds, did not typically offer him a Bible. Perhaps they anticipated Jalal would reject the offer with the objection that the Bible has been corrupted. Instead, the Christians he met talked about the Bible. Each time Jalal objected to their reasoning, they gave responses similar to the five arguments listed above.

Their reasoning always failed with Jalal. They were no match for his debating and reasoning skills, and the debates about the differences between Islam and Christianity were to no avail, like when Christians tried using the Quran 3.42–55 method described earlier in this chapter. Jalal pointed out, as Muslims familiar with the teachings of the Quran typically do, that this one passage is incomplete without the other twenty-four verses that refer to Jesus. The proper context of these verses, along with the others in the Quran, deny the deity of Jesus. The Quran actually teaches that to claim the Trinity or the deity of Christ is blasphemous, even an unforgiveable sin.

Jalal was not sure if these Christians were merely ignorant and ill-informed or whether they were purposely deceitful to twist and misapply the Quran in such ways. Regardless of their true motives, Jalal thought that if Christians twisted or misapplied the words of the

Quran to fit their view in such a manner, then how much more had they twisted and corrupted the Bible?

As is typical with Muslims, Jalal was suspicious of what Christians say and do. He already viewed Christians as ignorant of the truth and misguided spiritually. His encounter with these Christians made him even more leery of them, thinking they all must be deceived by the lies of Satan. At the same time, these encounters strengthened Jalal's resolve to try to save as many Christians as possible by helping convert them to Islam.

The Greatest Seed Ever

As was his custom on weekends, Jalal joined some of his Muslim friends for a fun game of soccer. One of the players who joined their game that weekend did not appear to be Muslim and had poor soccer skills. But this man, Mitch, was having lots of fun, and Jalal's Muslim friends seemed to enjoy his presence.

Curious, Jalal asked Mitch, "Are you Muslim?"

Mitch responded, "No, I'm Christian."

Jalal said, "Well, I'm glad you are here. You are most welcome to play soccer with us anytime. But I noticed your game needs much improvement. I've played soccer since I was a little boy. I will be glad to teach you a few things if you would like." Mitch agreed with enthusiasm.

Curious, Jalal later asked Mitch another question: "What motivated you, as a Christian, to be with all us Muslims?"

Mitch replied, "Jesus put His love for Muslims in my heart."

Jalal could not control his zeal, and he interrupted Mitch with, "We Muslims revere Jesus, peace be upon Him, as a messenger. As a matter of fact, Jesus, peace be upon Him, is mentioned more in the Quran than is Muhammad, peace be upon him. Christians think they need Jesus, peace be upon him, as Savior. Allah is most merciful and forgiving. Allah forgives us when we repent. But Allah's generosity is so great that we can attain it simply through our constant appeals for his mercy and forgiveness. Why do you Christians complicate God's forgiveness with things like the crucifixion?"

Mitch replied, "It is best that I read an answer to you right out of God's word as He revealed it in the Bible. I have a study Bible app on my phone. Let's look at the answer together."

Mitch then proceeded to open his Bible app on his smartphone and pulled up Romans 3:20–31 (NLT). I urge you to read the entire passage for yourself, but I will highlight some statements from this portion of scripture that provided a biblical answer to Jalal's question:

We are made right with God by placing our faith in Jesus Christ ... For everyone has sinned; we all fall short of God's glorious standard. Yet God, with undeserved kindness, declares that we are righteous. He did this through Christ Jesus when he freed us from the penalty for our sins. For God presented Jesus as the sacrifice for sin ... God did this to demonstrate his righteousness, for he himself is fair and just, and he declares sinners to be right in his sight when they believe in Jesus ... So, we are made right with God through faith and not by obeying the law.

Jalal stood speechless for a moment. Mitch then said, "God has answers to your questions in the Bible. And as you just saw, with a study Bible you can look up your questions or specific subjects and get thorough and in-depth answers directly from God." Mitch then proceeded to offer a study Bible to Jalal.

Jalal responded, "But the Bible has been corrupted—"

Mitch then interrupted Jalal. "Oh no, Jalal. God's word stands forever. Look at what the Bible states in Mark 13:31: 'Heaven and earth will disappear, but my words will never disappear' (NLT). This verse in the study Bible leads you to others like it throughout the Bible. I hope you accept my gift and read God's word in the Bible to discover His promises about His word."

Jalal accepted a Bible from Mitch and began a long journey of studying the Bible on his own. At first, Jalal viewed it as a challenge to find the corruption of the Bible. Jalal was confident he would find it, thus gaining a good tool to help him persuade Christians into converting to Islam. But as Jalal read the Bible, the Holy Spirit revealed the truth to him. It took two years, but Jalal accepted Jesus Christ as Lord and Savior. Jalal is now a Christian evangelist.

Mitch did with Jalal exactly what we teach at iHOPE workshops, which is to offer Muslims a Bible in whatever format and language is best suited for them and their situation—and to do so as soon as possible. This is the third of the five essentials.

Relying on God's Word

The greatest and most fruitful gospel seed ever in the history of the world is the word of God itself, the Bible! We will take a short pause from the stories to study three Bible passages that point us to the power of God's word. We will then resume with the stories to illustrate practical applications and adequately cover the main topics I promised you at the beginning of this chapter.

The Most Powerful Seed

> In the beginning, God created the heavens and the earth. The earth was without form and void, and darkness was over the face of the deep. And the Spirit of God was hovering over the face of the waters. And God said, 'Let there be light,' and there was light. (Genesis 1:1–3 ESV)

In Genesis 1, God spoke, and everything was created. God's word brought forth life. Human words—yours and mine—lack the life-giving power of God's word. The more we persuade or answer with *our* words, the more complicated and harder the work of sharing the gospel becomes. Moreover, we are planting weak seeds—gospel seeds that are diluted by our arguments and opinions—that are less impactful, producing the least fruit.

Meanwhile, the more we plant the actual word of God with a

Muslim, like Mitch did, the simpler and more doable, joyful, and fruitful our work will be because we are planting the most powerful seed.

Soul-Penetrating Seed

> For the word of God is alive and powerful. It is sharper than the sharpest two-edged sword, cutting between soul and spirit, between joint and marrow. It exposes our innermost thoughts and desires. (Hebrews 4:12 NLT)

God's word, the holy scriptures that comprise the Bible, penetrates the entirety of a person, mind, heart, soul, and spirit. God's word has living power. It penetrates and adapts to produce its intended effect on the person reading or hearing it. There can be no escape from the penetrating and searching power of the word of God.

God's word can force its way through all opposition, penetrating the hardest, most intimate, secret, and hidden parts of a person. It pierces the very essence of the soul. God's word reaches the heart, the very center of action, and lays open the motives and feelings of the person. It can expose and humble the proud. It can reveal the sinful soul, leading it into repentance. It pierces and awakens the conscience, convinces, and converts.

By relying more on their own words, it was as if Samira, Rahila, and Mahmoud were trying to penetrate hard hearts with wet noodles. In effect, their arguments complicated and diluted the seed they were trying to plant. They failed to realize (or remember) that Muslim apologetics address every conceivable Christian argument regarding the word of God.

Meanwhile, Mitch used the sword of the Spirit, the word of God, successfully planting this simple yet powerful seed, which penetrated Jalal's heart and soul. Mitch offered just a few of his own words to transition effectively to the Bible, and then he read scripture. In about five minutes, Mitch planted what Muslim apologetics cannot prepare for or stop, and that is the soul-penetrating word of God itself. There is no adequate human defense of any kind against the word of God. Mitch simply unleashed it and got out of the way.

Guaranteed Seed

> For as the rain and the snow come down from heaven and do not return there but water the earth, making it bring forth and sprout, giving seed to the sower and bread to the eater, so shall my word be that goes out from my mouth; it shall not return to me empty, but it shall accomplish that which I purpose, and shall succeed in the thing for which I sent it. (Isaiah 55:10–11 ESV)

God guarantees that His word accomplishes His intended purpose. In these verses, God likens His word to rain falling on the earth. The rain waters the earth, fertile and nonfertile soil alike. Only God's word can penetrate a hardened heart. For some, unfortunately, it is not to save them, but perhaps it is to give them access to the saving truth, giving them the opportunity to repent. In this way, God demonstrates that to all—those who accept and those who reject His word—His perfect justice, righteousness, mercy, and love.

The Most Fruitful Evangelistic Tool Ever

Through the years, I have personally heard hundreds of testimonies (and read hundreds more) of Christians from Muslim backgrounds. There are endless varieties to their testimonies, but except for a few, they all share a common thread: each one either read, viewed, or listened to a portion of the Bible. God's word was instrumental in their conversion. I know this is true for 100 percent of the thousands of Muslims who accepted Jesus as Lord and Savior through me, our ministry, our associates, and our partners. All of them studied some portion of the Bible before becoming believers. In terms of being wise or strategic with outreach efforts, the most fruitful thing you can do is give a Bible to a Muslim in whatever format and language is best suited for him or her.

Have you noticed? In every story I have shared with you in this book, the Christian person gave a Bible to a Muslim. It's a simple, doable, and duplicable action (just like every other of the five essentials). When you offer a Muslim a Bible as soon as is appropriate or possible, you are taking one of the most direct routes to finding a Muslim person of peace whose heart God has prepared to receive His word.

Now let's review four vital distinctions and practical applications we can learn from the stories shared in this chapter.

1. The Testimonies

Samira, Rahila, and Mahmoud consistently shared their testimonies with Muslims, but their words did not have the impact they desired. For a variety of reasons, testimonies tend not to resonate with Muslims. Of the hundreds of former Muslims I personally know, and the other hundreds of testimonies I know of, I do not recall any of them citing the testimony of a Christian, whether a former Muslim or otherwise, as influencing them to *seek* the Christian faith.

This isn't to say testimonies are useless or unimportant. I have, for example, observed how Christian testimonies can nudge a Muslim into accepting Jesus as Lord and Savior, but only after the Muslim was already on the verge of doing so; likewise, the testimonies of other Christians, especially those of former Muslims, do encourage and help solidify the faith of a former Muslim, especially that of brand-new Christians from Muslim backgrounds.

Part of the reason testimonies have negligible impact on Muslims as a means of moving them to seek Christ is that Muslims believe they already have the superior and only true religion (just as we Christians believe about our faith). Muslims react to Christian testimonies the same way you likely would if a Muslim shared his testimony with you. You would not be influenced to seek the Islamic faith.

With the typical Muslim reaction (or lack thereof) to testimonies in mind, it is needless to craft elaborate testimonies like Samira, Rahila, and Mahmoud did; moreover, Islamic apologetics prepare Muslims for testimonies of Christians. They may already have a pre-prepared answer or objection to your testimony, but remember, there is no adequate human defense for the actual word of God.

Did you notice in Mitch's story that he only shared a one-sentence testimony before Jalal interrupted him? Rather than trying to prepare a long, detailed testimony to share with the Muslims you meet, I recommend you have a short testimony ready. One short paragraph is adequate. You may even want to adapt Mitch's testimony.

Here's what he typically says: "Jesus put His love for Muslims in my heart. With all the terrorist attacks I hear about that are reported to be done by Islamic extremists, I used to be afraid of, angry with, even hated Muslims. But because Jesus lives in my heart, He put His love for Muslims in my heart. Now I seek Muslims so I can share the love of Jesus with them."

With Muslims, a short testimony is usually the best. One important reason for that, within the context of this chapter, is that it is best to plant the very word of God, the Bible, as soon as possible. Our own words are infinitely weaker in comparison with God's word, so it is best to keep them to a minimum and focus instead on what the Bible has to say.

Mitch's primary goal with his testimony is to introduce the Bible into his conversation as soon as possible. With Jalal, Mitch was looking for the Holy Spirit to open the door, and He did—even before Mitch could get his whole testimony out! That's when Mitch pointed to scripture and moved out of the way. Over a two-year period, God's word, not anyone else's, penetrated Jalal's previously hard heart and led him to recognize and accept Christ as his Lord and Savior.

As you reach out to Muslims, depend on God to help you find

a person of peace. He will lead you to a Muslim whose heart He has prepared for the gospel. Then, as soon as possible, and appropriate, plant the greatest and most fruitful gospel seed ever, which God put into the greatest and most fruitful gospel tool ever, the Bible. Relying on God and His word are the simplest and most effective things you can do with a Muslim.

2. Gospel Tailored to Muslims

Samira, Rahila, and Mahmoud shared the gospel with Muslims for several years with little fruit. Most of the words they used were their own, not directly from the Bible. They used highly intelligent illustrations and parables customized for Muslim audiences. They conveyed the gospel tailored to Muslims through them. Despite all their efforts and inside knowledge as former Muslims, very few Muslims believed in Christ.

As Jalal spoke to Mitch, he summarized some of the main reasons Muslims reject the good news of Jesus as Lord and Savior. In summary, Muslims believe God is most merciful and forgiving. God typically forgives the repentant. They do not see a need for Jesus dying on the cross for God to offer forgiveness. Samira, Rahila, and Mahmoud anticipated such objections and countered them with their illustrations, to no avail. The reason? Islamic apologists prepare Muslims to reject such illustrations.

In contrast, Mitch used two short sentences to transition to the Bible for the answer. Mitch shared the good news through the Bible itself in Romans 3:20–31. I have used this same passage with most of the two thousand Muslims with whom I have personally shared the gospel. We teach iHOPE workshop participants to do the same. Why? Because this passage offers the most fruitful gospel presentation we have ever seen with Muslims.

The reason Romans 3:20–31 is so effective with Muslims is multifaceted. The first, most obvious reason is the focus of this chapter: the Bible itself is sharing the gospel. Here God explains why Jesus had to die on the cross. These verses reveal the perfect balance of love, mercy, and justice that a holy, trustworthy, just, and righteousness God (Judge, Father, and Savior) must have to be all He claims to be.

Created beings are not capable of understanding any of this passage unless God helps us understand. Even then, as finite beings, we are capable of only comprehending a tiny bit of God's infinite truth. As we have studied in the Bible so far in this book, no amount of human reasoning can reveal any of this to anyone; only the Holy Spirit can.

So, it is best for us to simply do with Muslims what Mitch did with Jalal. Mitch did not try to answer Jalal's objections about the cross. Instead, Mitch pointed Jalal to these verses, which began a two-year journey of biblical study. It is worth repeating: there is no adequate human reasoning against the word of God. Our best strategy is to simply release the word of God and convey the gospel through words He inspired. There is no need to try to come up with the answers ourselves, or to create perfect or clever human reasoning to convey the gospel to Muslims.

With this God-dependent and simple approach, we have seen God produce amazing fruit! The harvest is plentiful because God has prepared the hearts of countless of Muslims for the greatest gospel seed ever, the Bible. It isn't complicated or difficult! Simply go out with another believer, give away Bibles, and follow up with the Muslims who accept one by offering to study the Bible with them.

3. Handling the "Bible Corrupted" Objection

Sincere Christians in the LEM category, like Sam from the previous chapter and Samira, Rahila, and Mahmoud from this one, believe it is necessary to overcome the "Bible has been corrupted" objection Muslims have *before* offering them one. They believe the Muslim won't accept their offer. Thus, they are ready to defend the authenticity of the Bible through apologetics, including original manuscript evidence, etc. Muslim apologists are ready for and prepare Muslims to handle such Christian apologetics.

Contrast that with how Mitch handled the situation. When Jalal confronted Mitch with the "Bible has been corrupted" objection, Mitch did not defend the Bible with manuscript evidence or difficult methods. If Mitch did, it would have been like a baby defending a fierce lion.

Instead, Mitch simply deferred to the Bible. He did the wisest thing possible by humbly recognizing the weakness of his words in comparison to God's word. Mitch allowed the Bible to defend itself, and he offered Jalal a Bible. Within a minute of Mitch's offer, Jalal accepted a Bible. God is most able and most suited to defend His word. Remember, God's word is the one thing that penetrates the deepest parts of the heart, mind, and soul. God guarantees His word will accomplish His purpose. There are no adequate human defenses or apologetics (Islamic or otherwise) that can prevent God's word from doing His will.

When I first began reaching out to Muslims, I attempted to use the strategy of the LEM. I studied hard to gain the knowledge necessary to defend the Bible. I amassed overwhelming evidence to attest to its authenticity, and as I confronted Muslims with the evidence, they would refer to something in their holy books that I did not know. So I would go study more, diving deeper into specialized knowledge of Islam and their holy books. But it was never enough to anticipate the variety of counterarguments I heard.

Like so many in the LEM, I spent a tremendous amount of time debating with a few Muslims. Even though I gained enough knowledge and skill to feel like I won the debates, rarely did a Muslim accept a Bible from me, and the approach produced little fruit.

Through these least fruitful experiences, God taught me the lessons I am sharing with you. I made the necessary adjustments to my approach. I stopped defending the Bible and instead, unleashed it on the attackers, allowing it to defend itself. Like Mitch and others in the MEM, I only use the Bible to defend the Bible.

Note: Just as I shared earlier about personal testimonies, I discovered that there is a proper time and place for introducing the overwhelming evidence that supports the authenticity of the Bible. This apologetics defense does not typically persuade a Muslim to accept a Bible. But after God has already prepared their hearts so they accept a Bible, the manuscript evidence helps minimize the doubts and strengthen the faith of new believers and can nudge a Muslim seeker into becoming a believer.

4. Handling Objections of Muslims

Muslims have countless objections to Christianity. One of the most common ones concerns the Trinity. Most Muslims believe Christians worship three gods, which is considered a blasphemous, even unforgiveable sin. Samira, Rahila, and Mahmoud, like so many of the LEM do, used various illustrations to explain the Trinity, such as H_2O. With experience, they discovered, as I did early on when I used such illustrations, that these do not typically resonate with Muslims.

Mitch did not have to address this objection with Jalal, but he modeled the best path to address any Islamic objection: Refer to the Bible for answers. It is always best to use God's word to provide answers instead of our own.

You can expect to hear the Trinity objection when you talk with Muslims. The following story reveals how I handle this common objection.

Charles, one of our evangelistic partners, was overwhelmed with the large numbers of Muslims who had accepted Bibles from him and begun Bible studies with him. During one of my regular visits with Charles, I offered to help him a bit. Charles told me there were two Muslim men in the area we would be visiting that he suspected were radical, even potential terrorists. On previous visits, the two had attempted to intimidate Charles to stop reaching out to Muslims.

Charles warned me that they would probably show up while we were in the area, and they did. Charles asked me if I was willing to talk with them, so he could focus on the Muslim persons of peace God had led him to.

The two combative Muslims looked to be about twenty-five years of age. They approached us fast and appeared angry. I smiled and extended my arm for a handshake, but they did not extend theirs.

One of them said with a loud voice, “Are you with Charles?”

“Yes. My name is Renod. What is yours?” I replied.

He responded with a question: “Are you a Christian too?”

I replied, “Yes—”

Before I could say another word, he interrupted. “You and Charles need to stop committing blasphemy and to immediately stop from trying to have Muslims blaspheme with you.”

I asked, “How are we blaspheming?”

With even angrier and more intense tone, he said, “You worship three gods. And now you and Charles are here trying to lure Muslims away from the worship of the one and only Allah into worshiping the Christian Trinity. This is an unpardonable sin punishable by death.”

I responded, “Oh, no. We worship only one God. The Bible is very clear on that point. Here, look.” I opened the Bible to Romans 3:30 (ESV) and read the first four words: “Since God is one.” (Note: The Romans 3:20–31 passage not only points Muslims to the biblical teaching of only one God but also often draws them into the rest of the passage that shares the gospel in a Muslim-friendly way.)

Then I said, “You can search for yourself the word of God in the Bible to see what God has to say about any subject. You can also clarify the misunderstanding about Christians worshiping three gods.” They stood before me silently, as if processing what I just shared, so I continued.

“Look again here,” I said, pointing to Deuteronomy 6:4–5: “The Lord our God, the Lord is one. You shall love the Lord your God will all your heart and with all your soul and with all your might.”

They remained silent, so I continued to share, this time from Mark 12:29–30 (ESV): “The Lord our God, the Lord is one. And you shall love the Lord your God with all your heart and with all your soul and with all your mind and with all your strength."

I then offered both of them Bibles, and one accepted it. I then invited both to join us for a Bible study we were about to have. One just walked away slowly and quietly, as if he was stunned. Tarik, the one who accepted the Bible, joined us for the group Bible study.

I share the story to demonstrate the effectiveness of using the Bible to handle objections and to answer the toughest Islamic questions, even of radicals. The Trinity is typically the most difficult question to answer. How can you and I, created and finite beings, adequately explain the Creator, infinite God?

I have encountered countless objections to the Christian faith from Muslims, and I use the same strategy every time. Even when I know the answer and could just share it with them, I do not. Instead, I point them to a Bible, so they can see or hear the answer for themselves. Then I offer them a Bible (a study Bible if possible).

Our job is to say as little as necessary with our human words and let almighty God speak to them through His word. It is the simplest, least stressful, most doable, most duplicable, smartest, wisest, most loving, best strategic, and most fruitful thing to do.

Whatever the objection, there is no reason to try to anticipate one or be stressed about knowing the answer. It is simple to use a study Bible to find verses about the subject and get answers. It is best to empower your Muslim person of peace to find the answers directly from God's word.

If you do not have a study Bible, purchase a printed one, or download one to your computer, tablet, or smartphone. A study Bible typically comes with instructions on how to use it. Get comfortable using a study Bible, and then you can show your Muslim person of peace how to use it as well. You can search for a study Bible by looking on the internet with a search phrase like "study Bible app," and you'll get many results. You can also search for a "study Bible" book in the same way. You can even specify the language you're seeking. If you're looking for Bibles in many languages, written, oral, or dramatized, then I'll reference one I use: Bible.is. It's available in many languages and formats.

Back to the Three

Through a set of unique circumstances (orchestrated by God) Samira, Rahila, and Mahmoud ended up attending iHOPE workshops. It was the turning point for the three. They eventually embraced the biblical teachings of the five essentials for every Christian to know and do with Muslims. As a result, they became fruitful and are multiplying spiritually with Muslims worldwide.

Planting Seeds Where Terrorists Roam

Marissa is a brilliant young lady from a Christianized nation. She has a driven personality, exceptional character, and a strong work ethic that could help her succeed in any number of careers. She is also tall and blessed with such extreme physical beauty that she could have pursued a modeling career.

But Marissa's greatest love is God. While in college, she came to understand that God's purpose for her was to be help others know Him. After much prayer, she decided to move to an Islamic nation that is considered to be one of the most dangerous places on earth. That nation is a terrorist recruiting and training haven. Sharing of the gospel is illegal there. When Marissa went, there were no known Christians there; it's believed that it's 100 percent Muslim.

Marissa was part of a small team of Christians who were going to this Islamic nation to be ambassadors for Christ. While there, Marissa was paired up with Tami, another young Christian lady, to help tutor Muslim girls and women. Even though Marissa covered her body, wearing the traditional clothing expected of a Muslim woman, her height and light skin made her stand out.

Ruth and James, a married couple, left their Christianized nation to go to the same Islamic country. As Christian doctors, they went to areas where the people needed medical help but did not have access to it. Those areas were often the most dangerous, war-torn parts of the country.

In such places and situations, Muslims often ask the Christians something like this: "Why would you leave your wealthy and safe Christian country and risk your life coming to a very poor and dangerous Islamic country to be with us Muslims?"

In our iHOPE workshops and trainings, we teach Christians to respond this way: "God loves you, and He put His love for you in my heart. I would like to share with you what God's original word, the Bible, states in 2 Corinthians 5:11–21 (NLT). I will share only some of it: 'Christ's love controls us … God, who brought us back to himself through Christ. And God has given us this task of reconciling people to him. For God was in Christ, reconciling the world to himself, no longer counting people's sins against them. And he gave us this wonderful message of reconciliation. So, we are Christ's ambassadors; God is making His appeal through us.'"

And of course, the next step is to ask the Muslim if she or he would like a Bible to examine the rest of God's appeal and story.

Ruth, James, Marissa, Tami, and the rest of the teams they were a part of sought persons of peace to whom they could secretly give Bibles that were translated in the language of that Islamic country.

As Ruth and James did this, they were discovered and attacked by Islamic terrorists in the area. James died. Ruth survived. Local Muslims snuck her out of the area and helped her return to her Christianized nation, where she sought healing and recovery.

In the meantime, in a different area of that same country, Marissa and Tami were also discovered by terrorists. But instead of killing them, these terrorists kidnapped and imprisoned Marissa and Tami. The government of that country, with its weak and small military, did eventually find the terrorist hideout. Miraculously, the terrorists did not kill Marissa and Tami before fleeing.

Marissa, Tami, and Ruth left the country before they could see if the Bible seeds they and James had planted would produce any harvest. Many of their friends and loved ones in their Christianized countries questioned the wisdom of their decision to risk so much to go to that Islamic country in the first place.

A few years after her husband was murdered by Islamic terrorists, I heard Ruth share their testimony with a group of Christians. Ruth said that she is following through with what began with her deceased husband and that she would do it again and again. She continues to travel back to that Islamic country to encourage and disciple Christians from Muslim backgrounds to be fruitful and multiply. Yes, praise God, there are now some Christians there from Muslim backgrounds.

A few years after her kidnapping, Marissa shared her testimony with a group of Christians in a Christianized nation. Afterward, a man from the audience, Usman, approached Marissa and told her that he was one of the terrorists who had imprisoned her. Usman asked for Marissa's forgiveness and went on to share how she had impacted his life.

When Usman was with the terrorist group that kidnapped Marissa, they found Bibles with them, *and he secretly took one*. He said that initially he was not planning to read it. But the godly way Marissa and Tami handled the kidnapping ordeal moved him. Their behavior and continued display of faith led him to begin secretly reading the Bible. Usman knew some of the identities of the people who had Bibles from the team Marissa was originally with, and he connected with some.

Usman eventually accepted Jesus as his Lord and Savior. He met with other new Christians and formed underground house churches. Because that Islamic nation's government had never suspected or flagged Usman as a terrorist, he was able to get a visa to enter the Christianized nation where Marissa happened to be speaking that day.

He told Marissa that he was in the process of getting a seminary degree. Once he completed his studies, he would return to his home country to help grow the churches and discipleship movements that are forming there.

Risking It All for God's Glory

Marissa, Tami, Ruth, James, and the rest of the team members were not gifted as preachers. But they went to an Islamic country as ambassadors for Christ to use their God-given talents for the benefits of all. When spiritual conversations came up—and they are guaranteed to come up with Muslims—they looked for opportunities to secretly give Bibles to persons of peace. It was risky, and James was murdered for it. But the result of their faithfulness to plant the gospel seed is that Muslims in this dangerous country are coming to faith in Christ in unprecedented numbers.

A similar thing happened around two thousand years ago when a faithful few told the world about Jesus. That message has been transforming the world for Christ ever since. We can do the same with the Islamic world today. Even the hearts of terrorists can be transformed when obedient followers of Jesus use their God-given talents to seek out persons of peace and plant the greatest seed ever.

In Matthew 19:29 (NLT), Jesus said, "And everyone who has given up houses or brothers or sisters or father or mother or children or property, for my sake, will receive a hundred times as much in return and will inherit eternal life."

Where Sharing the Gospel Is Illegal

Darren is a printer by trade. He is a Christian who had a successful printing business in a Christianized nation. When he became aware of God's purpose for his life, he began seeking ways to be more fruitful. He took his printing business into a large Islamic country where sharing the gospel is illegal. There he specialized in printing material and literature in English. His business was successful, but his primary goal was to make Bibles available to Muslims.

Darren identified himself as a Christian so Muslims there would know him as such. Darren's business was close to an Islamic seminary.

One day, Adnan, a student at the seminary, asked Darren if he knew how he could get a Bible.

Adnan was a devout Muslim studying to become an Islamic scholar. He had a strong desire to come to a Christianized nation, where he could use his knowledge and skills to convert Christians to Islam. In all his preparations to do so, Adnan had not come across a Bible but was taught that it had been corrupted. Adnan thought that if he was to reason Christians away from the Bible and into the Quran, then he should know what the Bible actually teaches.

Adnan sought a Bible for months but could not find one. When someone told him that his best chance at finding one was to ask a Christian foreigner, he went to Darren, who happily provided him with a Bible.

Now that he had it, Adnan was terrified of reading the Bible! He was afraid of being possessed by evil spirits just for touching the Bible, let alone reading it. Adnan prayed that God would protect him if he was to read it. After three months of praying, Adnan felt courage and assurance to proceed and read the Bible. He first read the entire New Testament within one day. Then he read the whole Bible from cover to cover.

After about four months of studying the Bible on his own, Adnan was convinced that it was the true word of God. For days he prayed, crying and pleading with God to confirm the truth to him. Adnan finally surrendered his will to God, recognized the truth of the Bible, and accepted Christ as Lord and Savior.

Adnan has committed the rest of his life to leading Muslims to Jesus. He works full time in his native Islamic country to spark a discipleship and church-planting movement. Adnan loves his Islamic country and the Muslim people. His prayer is that God will use him to help transform his nation for Christ.

God used Darren to provide a Bible to Adnan. Darren used his God-given talent as a Christian businessperson to attract a Muslim person of peace whose heart God was preparing to receive His word. Darren merely planted the greatest gospel seed ever and did so in a legal way. Only the Lord of the harvest knows the future impact Darren's faithful obedience will have.

Where It Is illegal—a Christian Military Couple

Jerry and Lindsey are a young Christian couple in the military. After finishing their military service, Jerry became a security consultant, while Lindsey stayed home to raise their young children. As a family, they desired to fulfill God's purpose for their lives to make God known to others—and they felt a special pull to share the gospel with Muslims.

Jerry got a job in an Islamic country to help protect its people from the constant and various threats of Islamic extremists and terrorists. Although it is illegal in that country to share the gospel for the purpose of converting a Muslim into Christianity, Christian foreigners can gather and worship in private.

One Sunday during the group's worship service, Saad knocked at the door of the house. Saad asked, "I would like a Bible so I can read and understand what Christians believe. May I get one from you?"

The Christian pastor of the small church refused to give Saad a Bible. He questioned Saad, fearful that he was a spy for the government or one of the Islamic extremist groups that wanted to persecute Christians. Every Christian in that small church—except Lindsey and Jerry—fearfully doubted Saad's motives and supported the pastor in refusing to give him a Bible.

Lindsey and Jerry understood that it would have been illegal for them to share the gospel with Saad to convert him to Christianity, but they would have done it anyway had they been directed by God to do so. In this case, they didn't have to break the law. They did the legal thing that also happens to be the best way to share the gospel: they gave Saad the Bible he requested. They did not know Saad's true motives, but they knew the power of God's word.

Saad was not a government spy, nor did he belong to an Islamic extremist group. God had been preparing Saad's heart for the gospel for a long time. As a result, the desire in Saad's heart had intensified to the point that he was willing to risk his own life by approaching the Christian group and asking for a Bible to study.

Every day more Christians are discovering that God has been doing the same with countless Muslims. We simply need more Christians who, like Lindsey and Jerry, are willing to faithfully fulfill God's second primary purpose to be fruitful and multiply with Muslims. You'll notice that Lindsey and Jerry didn't go out looking to convert Muslims in the Islamic country where they lived. They simply made themselves available among Muslims and followed the opportunities God created. They did not preach, nor did they use complicated methodologies or complex arguments; they merely gave a Muslim a Bible. And because of their faithfulness and the power of God's word, Saad accepted Jesus as his Lord and Savior, as did his wife and children.

Today there are reports of hundreds of underground house groups where Muslims are studying the Bible, establishing secret churches, and creating discipleship groups that encourage new Christians to continue to multiply. Most of these Muslims did not know each other at first, and they did not know that other Muslims were also seeking to know the truth about God and His Son. Like Saad, they typically have a tough time finding a Bible or a Christian who is willing to give them a Bible or study it with them. But when the greatest seed took root in their hearts, the gospel thrived.

Impacting Our Futures

Christians in Jerry and Lindsey's church, in an Islamic country where the gospel is illegal, responded to a Muslim with fear. It is understandable to experience fear in situations like this one, but our fear does not negate our responsibility to obey God. Can you imagine if the followers of Jesus would have responded in a similar way when they encountered persecution? The gospel was also illegal then, and those who dared to believe in Christ risked their lives to share it.

The orders of the authorities then conflicted with God's orders, so Christians disobeyed earthly rulers and obeyed God instead. As Jesus commanded, they followed Him to the cross instead of running away from it.

God has redeemed us to redeem the world through us. God empowered us with His word and with the Holy Spirit, which means we have everything we need to accomplish our callings and fulfill God's purposes for our lives.

When we disobey God in being fruitful and multiplying with Muslims, we face the reality that future generations will live in Islamic nations—worldwide. But if we obey God's command, like Lindsey and Jerry chose to do, we can help change the trajectory of the future for the generations to come.

The five essentials for every Christian to know and do with Muslims are simple, doable, and duplicable. First, we must understand God's primary purposes for our lives: to know Him and make Him known. That means being willing to share the gospel. Next, we must submit to the Holy Spirit's power and direction by seeking persons of peace, those people whose hearts He has prepared to receive the gospel seed. Then, when we find a person of peace, the third essential is to simply offer him or her a Bible.

Every Christian you know and everyone in your church can get involved in this mission to share the love and hope of Christ with Muslims. We can do it in our neighborhoods, cities, and nations and around the world. God guarantees His word will succeed in accomplishing His purposes. God has called us all to spread His word. Our future generations need us to answer the call.

Note: You can research study Bibles online. You will find print ones to purchase and apps for smart devices or computers. You can do similar online searches for audio and dramatized Bibles in thousands of languages. One unique and immensely helpful resource is bible.is.

CHAPTER 10
The Fourth Essential: Pray with Them

We have covered three of the five essentials of sharing the gospel with Muslims. We know the greatest seed to sow with Muslims is the word of God—the Bible. But is there a way to nourish that seed and help it grow into a fruitful harvest?

Yes!

In this chapter, we'll look at a seldom-used nutrient that can help the seed grow and flourish. Islamic apologists cannot defend against it, and it is one of the simplest and most effective things you and I can do. This nutrient can be used anywhere in the world; there is not a place on earth (that I am aware of) where it is illegal. The following is a story that illustrates the fourth of the five essentials that every Christian must know and do with Muslims.

Miraculous Healing

Dalilah is a beautiful and intelligent young woman who was born and raised in a devout, wealthy Muslim family in an Islamic country. From her childhood, Dalilah suffered with symptoms that caused her parents to believe she was possessed by a demon. Dalilah always felt sad and fatigued. She did not enjoy life at all, and she became a recluse. She could muster just enough energy to go to school and do homework. But apart from school, she slept the rest of the time, including entire weekends. Dalilah felt so empty, and all these things led her to have recurring suicidal thoughts. Her parents sought help for Dalilah, and she was eventually diagnosed with clinical depression. Her doctors prescribed a variety of medications, all of which came with awful side effects.

Dalilah and her parents prayed persistently for healing, the usual five times per day for Muslims, but Dalilah was not healed. They asked Islamic religious leaders and the Islamic community to pray over her and on her behalf, but Dalilah was not healed. Then Dalilah and her parents increased their daily prayers up to twelve times daily, and still Dalilah was not healed.

Despite her depression, Dalilah did extremely well in school and was ranked in the top tier of her class. Witnessing her academic success, Dalilah's parents thought that if she were to study overseas, perhaps the change of scenery would improve her symptoms. They trusted Dalilah's character, morals, and Islamic roots enough to send her to a Christianized nation where she would have greater educational opportunities and be able to maximize her potential.

Dalilah was stressed about moving alone overseas, especially to a Christianized nation. She knew of a few Christians in her Islamic country, but they had never interacted with her. Nevertheless, Dalilah moved into a Christianized nation as an international student but remained a recluse.

Kari and Dalilah

Kari, a dentist, is a Christian who desires to fulfill God's purpose for her life. To increase her opportunity to meet non-Christians, she volunteered as a language conversational partner at the university where Dalilah was attending. Kari prayed to meet international students with whom she could seek opportunities to share the good news of Jesus.

Kari noticed Dalilah sitting alone at lunch one day, looking sad. She decided to talk with her, and very shortly into the conversation, Dalilah burst into tears. It took a while, but Dalilah composed herself and shared her plight with Kari. The move away from all her loved ones and support system into a new country, combined with clinical depression, was proving too much for Dalilah.

As Kari listened, she felt compelled to pray for Dalilah—not just silently, but aloud—with her. Kari offered to pray for the young woman and first explained that, as a Christian, she would end the prayer by appealing to God in the name of Jesus.

Dalilah explained right back to Kari that she was a Muslim, and she and her parents had been praying for help and healing—up to twelve times daily—since Dalilah was around seven years old. But Dalilah thought, *Why not? Another prayer, even by a Christian, could not hurt.* She then accepted Kari's offer to pray for her in the name of Jesus.

They closed their eyes and bowed their heads, and Kari prayed for Dalilah, asking God to at least help her feel better, but perhaps even heal her, if it was His will. Then Kari said, "In Jesus's name, amen."

What Is Happening to Me?

After the prayer, Dalilah sat silently and looked bewilderedly at Kari. Slowly, she began to smile. Then the smile turned into laughter. Then she jumped out of her seat and kept jumping up and down. She tried to explain to Kari what she was feeling, but it was difficult, because Dalilah could not remember another time in her life when she had ever smiled or laughed or felt so energized!

Dalilah told Kari that at the moment she said, "In Jesus's name," she saw in her mind what looked like the hand of God gently reaching inside of her and removing her heavy and dark heart. At that moment, she felt sadness and depression instantly leave her body. And in the next moment, she saw the same hand, in the same gentle manner, putting a new, bright, healthy heart into her. She instantly began to feel happy, which led her to smile and laugh uncontrollably. She felt energized, as if her new heart was pumping super energy into her entire being.

For fifteen years, she and her parents had prayed in mosques daily, many times a day. Islamic religious leaders had spoken words from the Quran over her, and the entire Islamic community around her prayed on her behalf—but she was not healed. But when Kari prayed in Jesus's name, Dalilah felt changed instantly.

Tell Me about Him

In Dalilah's mind and heart, Jesus was the difference maker, and she wanted to know more about Him. Kari pointed Dalilah to the Bible and several passages (Romans 3:20–31; 10:8–13; Ephesians 2:4–10) to share the gospel with her. Dalilah immediately accepted Jesus as her Lord and Savior.

Of the thousands of Muslims I know of who have come to faith in Christ, Dalilah was the quickest to do so. Nine months after Dalilah accepted Christ, I met her at a discipleship conference tailored for former Muslims. Dalilah told me she hadn't needed to take any depression-related medicines since that miraculous day Kari had prayed for her. From how joyful, warm, and friendly that Dalilah was, I would have never guessed she was formerly clinically depressed.

Dalilah told me that her family in their Islamic country had disowned her. She went from material wealth to financial poverty. She also told me that Jesus was worth it. She now has an eternal wealth that no one can ever take from her.

Dalilah's story is an example of the fourth essential for every Christian to know and do with Muslims: praying with a Muslim in the name of Jesus—and to do so as soon as possible.

Many Christians pray for Muslims and their salvation, and I hope that they and you continue to do so. But the fourth of the five essentials is about praying *with*—not just for—Muslims in the name of Jesus, just as Kari did with Dalilah.

Prayer in Jesus's name is one of the most God-centered, God-dependent, God-glorifying things we can do. It is also one of the most effective ways I have ever seen to lift up the name of Jesus with a Muslim. It is the greatest gospel-seed nutrient ever, helping the gospel seed come to fruition. This is exactly what happened when Kari prayed with Dalilah.

For Kari, praying in Jesus's name made Christ the primary focus. Kari lifted up Jesus in the simplest way possible. The prayer wasn't long or complicated; she did not expect or anticipate a miracle. She merely knew that it is always a good idea to pray and to do so in the name of Jesus, especially with a non-Christian. Kari had to depend on God to answer the prayer as He saw best fit, and whatever the answer, God would receive all the credit.

For Dalilah, Jesus was the difference maker. The miraculous answer to Kari's prayer glorified Jesus and God with Dalilah—and the same is true for many former Muslims.

Do Miracles Still Happen?

You may be wondering if miracles still happen. It's a question I am asked often. I can't tell you when or where miracles will happen, but I can tell you that an honest prayer in Jesus's name often precedes undeniably supernatural happenings.

I have prayed in the name of Jesus with more than twelve hundred Muslims. Many of the prayers included requests for miraculous results. I have witnessed eleven miracles and heard of others. That means that I witnessed less than 1 percent of my prayer requests for Muslims result in miracles. So over 99 percent of the time when and where I was involved, there was not a physical or known miracle. But most often, miracle or not, something awesome still happened with the Muslims with whom I've prayed. The following is a story that illustrates that.

Steph was born into a devout Muslim family in an Islamic country in the Middle East. A birth defect left her severely handicapped, paralyzed from the neck down. Despite her tiny, deformed body, Steph's mind was healthy and intelligent. Her big, beautiful eyes communicated love, peace, joy, and inner strength all at the same.

Steph loved to sing, and her ever-present smile brightened every place she went.

Steph's family had prayed more than five times per day since her birth. They, Islamic religious leaders, and the Islamic community around them begged God to miraculously heal Steph, but she was not healed.

Refugees Fleeing Islamic War

When Steph was seventeen years old, an Islamic war erupted in her birth country. Her father left Steph and her mom to become a jihadist in the war. Her uncle also left her aunt to join the war efforts.

With their own lives at risk, Steph, her mother, and her aunt fled the country. They had to leave everything behind except the clothes on their backs and Steph's wheelchair. They sought refuge in a neighboring Middle Eastern country and were taken into a tent city established for refugees, about seven miles away from the border of Steph's birth country. They were grateful to be away from the raging war, but they were also scared to be within miles of it. Every day they heard explosions and automatic machine-gun fire. In fear, they listened to the sounds of battle to determine whether the battle was getting closer. They felt helpless since they did not have a vehicle or a way of escape if war ever did reach the refugee camp.

Although they were removed from the immediate threat of violence, their lives were far from easy. They lived in horrible, unsanitary conditions with no running water, kitchen, bathroom, or shower. Their new tent home, of course, had no heating and offered very little protection from the heat of the day. And without enough blankets to keep them warm through the cold nights, their living conditions were extremely poor. One of their greatest fears was getting sick or needing medical attention. Part-time volunteers offered the only medical assistance, and with limited supplies available, they knew sickness could very well end in death. As was their custom, they continued to pray five times per day or more, making additional appeals for the end of the wars and the safe return of Steph's father and uncle. They also begged God for improved economic and living conditions.

Out of Tent City

One day, a Christian man named Khalil visited the refugee tent city to see how he could help. While there, he met Steph and her family and told them he could get Steph's mom and aunt low-wage jobs in a big city about forty miles from the tent city.

Steph was nineteen, and Kahlil was the first Christian she had met. None of the few Christian neighbors in her home country had ever interacted with her, and she had certainly never heard the good news of Jesus Christ from them. Steph only knew Christians as infidels and had a negative impression of them. So imagine the confusion she felt when this Christian man offered his help.

Steph's mom and aunt pooled their meager wages, thus affording a small studio apartment where they lived in a slum-like area of the city. The tiny, one-room apartment was pitiful, but at least it had a kitchen and bathroom. The room provided more warmth than a tent in the cold winter nights and was a bit cooler through the hot summer. Such small comforts were significant improvements over living in a tent home.

In the meantime, they still had no news from Steph's dad or uncle. Steph prayed they were still alive but wondered how they would find each other, as they had no means of communication. Steph, her mom, and her aunt sunk deeper into hopelessness, with no end in sight for the harsh life of refugees in the Middle East.

House Church

Khalil told them about a place not too far from them where a few Christians prayed with and for Muslims for miracles from God. When they heard that God sometimes answered prayers there and some miracles had been reported, Steph's mom and aunt put her in the wheelchair and made the long walk to the meeting place—a house-turned-church in a poverty-stricken neighborhood.

They met several Christians there who seemed nice and loving—and quite different from the lifelong negative perceptions Steph had had of Christians in general. The leaders of this small group of Christians were a couple, John and Mary, from a Christianized nation. They had both graduated from college with seminary degrees and then moved from their Western nation to be long-term missionaries in this Islamic country in MENA. They knew a little bit of Arabic but not adequately enough to lead the communication in the meetings. The main communicators were an Arabic Christian couple, Elie and Perla.

Elie was a high school dropout who had begun working in construction as a teenager. Perla was also a high school dropout who worked in a beauty parlor. They grew up in Christian homes, but neither one of them were believers when they got involved in drugs as teenagers, met each other, and got married in their early twenties. They had children, which added to the pressure Elie felt as a provider, a husband, and a father. So Elie began consuming more drugs and became physically abusive with Perla. That's when Perla left Elie and took the kids with her. In the crisis, Elie turned to a Christian friend he knew, and he helped lead Elie to Christ as his Lord and Savior. God transformed Elie. Seeing the transformation in Elie, Perla herself surrendered her life to Christ, and the family was reunited. Elie became a full-time worker in the ministry under the leadership of John. Perla continues to work full time in the beauty parlor and serves in the ministry alongside Elie on nights and weekends.

The church meetings began with a Christian prayer that concluded with, "in the name of Jesus, amen." These prayers were unlike what Steph's family had ever seen, heard, or prayed themselves.

The Daily Islamic Prayer

Steph's family prayed the traditional, ritualistic Muslim prayer at least five times per day. The Islamic prayer ritual lasts around five minutes, and typically is the following prayer:

> Allah is the greatest. Allah is the greatest. I bear witness that there is none worthy of worship, save Allah. I bear witness that Muhammad is the messenger of Allah. Come to prayer. Come to prosperity. The prayer is ready. Allah is the greatest. Allah is the greatest. There is none worthy of worship, save Allah. I have turned my full attention towards him, who has created the heavens and the earth, being ever inclined towards him. And I am not among those who associate partners with Allah. Allah is the greatest. Glory to thee, o Allah, praiseworthy and blessed is the name and exalted is the majesty, and there is no one worthy of worship except thee alone. I seek refuge with Allah from Satan, the accursed. In the name of Allah, the gracious, the merciful. All praise belongs to Allah, Lord of all worlds. The gracious, the merciful, master of the Day of Judgment. Thee alone do we worship, and thee alone do we implore for help. Guide us on the right path. The path of those upon whom thou hast bestowed thy blessings. Not of those who have incurred they displeasure, nor of those who have gone astray. Amen. Allah, the one. He begets not, nor is he begotten, and there's none like unto him. Allah is the greatest. Holy is my lord, the most great. Holy is my lord, the most great. Holy is my lord, the most great. Allah hears him who praises him. O, our lord, and thine is the praise. The praise which

> is plenty, pure, and blessed. Allah is the greatest. Holy is my lord, the most high. Holy is my lord, the most high. Holy is my lord, the most high. Allah is the greatest. O Allah, forgive me, and have mercy on me, and make good for me my shortcoming, and guide me, and grant me security, and make good for me my shortcoming, and provide for me. Allah is the greatest. Holy is my lord, the most great. Holy is my lord, the most great. Holy is my lord, the most great. Allah is the greatest. All verbal and physical acts of worship and financial sacrifices are due to Allah. Peace be on you, o Prophet, and the mercy of Allah and his blessings. Peace be on us, and on the righteous servants of Allah. Allah is the greatest. And I bear witness that Muhammad is his servant and his messenger. Bless, o Allah, Muhammad and his people as thou didst bless Abraham and his people. Thou art indeed praiseworthy, the exalted. Our lord, bestow on us good in this world, and good in the hereafter, and shield us from the torment of the fire. My lord, make me observe prayer and my children too. Our lord, bestow thy grace on me and accept my prayer. Our lord, grant forgiveness to me and to my parents, and to the believers on the day of the reckoning. Peace be on you, and the blessings of Allah. Peace be on you, and the blessings of Allah.

New Experiences

Steph's family were very attracted to the Christian prayers at the house church meetings. They found themselves desiring more of them. They felt free to pray what was on their heart. Like many of the other Muslims that keep coming back for prayers in Jesus's name, they said they felt hope, peace, and joy praying there.

Then, at their first house church gathering, Steph witnessed and heard something strange and new to her: worship music. You see, Muslims do not sing or have any type of music for prayers or worship. Steph's family loved the lyrics of the worship songs. Steph was surprised when some of the other Muslims in the church joined the Christian leader in singing, and she was overjoyed when she was told she could sing along.

Then Elie began reading aloud from the Bible, John 3:1–15. Steph was intrigued by it all. She heard things she never heard before, like verse 3 (ESV): "Unless one is born again he cannot see the kingdom of God." Steph desired to hear more. But when Elie read John 3:16 (ESV), "For God so loved the world, that he gave his only Son, that whoever believes in him should not perish but have eternal life," Steph's world seemed to go silent.

You see, Steph had prayed the Muslim prayer more than five times per day since she was a little girl. That prayer typically included the line from the Islamic prayer I shared with you above: "Allah, the one. He begets not, nor is he begotten, and there's none like unto him."

Gospel for the First Time

Steph instantly rejected the part about "His only Son" as blasphemy. You see Muslims typically reject the idea of Jesus being God's Son. Many mistakenly think Christians believe that God had an intimate physical relation with Mary and that Jesus was born as a result. Steph thought, like many Muslims do, that Christians worship three gods: God the Father, Mary the mother, and Jesus the Son. To Muslims, this belief is blasphemy and an unpardonable sin.

But another part of the verse did resonate with Steph: "For God so loved the world." Like many other Muslims, Steph knew the ninety-nine names Islam has for God, but love was not one of them. Despite her confusion and apprehension about the verse she had heard, Steph felt an overwhelming desire to know this loving God. When Elie offered her a Bible, Steph accepted wholeheartedly, as did her mom and aunt.

For the first time in their lives, Steph, her mom, and her aunt heard the good news about Jesus. They rejected Him as Lord and Savior but began taking turns reading the Bible.

Angry Muslim Man

After the Bible teaching part of the meeting, the Christians asked the dozens of Muslims in the packed house to come forward if they wanted special prayers in the name of Jesus. A very angry-looking Muslim man in the crowd, Amir, stood up. Amir's right arm had been crushed and paralyzed from a severe auto accident. Amir was already financially poor, and the injury to his arm made him unemployable, increasing his financial woes and anger.

Like Steph, Amir had an extremely negative perception of Christians and thought of them as infidels. Prior to that house church meeting that day, he had never heard the good news about Jesus. Like Steph and her family, he rejected the ideas of Jesus as Lord and Savior, but because he was desperate for a miracle, Amir accepted the offer to be prayed over in the name of Jesus.

Following the prayer, Amir's paralyzed arm was healed instantly. In shock and amazement, he began to test his arm by moving it in every way possible. Yes, it was healed, and he had full range of motion. He and Steph, along with dozens of Muslims in the church that night, witnessed a miracle from God. In shocked gratitude, Amir leapt around the room praising God. In response to his miracle, Amir accepted Jesus as Lord and Savior. Seeing his healing and joy, Steph's family rushed forward seeking a miracle for Steph, but unlike Amir, she was not healed.

Steph discovered that the Christians held two of these services in the house each week, along with daily Bible studies. They began attending both services each week with the dozens of other Muslims they met there, everyone seeking miracles from God. For months, they kept coming multiple times per week, worshiping, studying the Bible, and praying, but Steph was not healed.

Angelic Voice

A few months later, my wife and I took a small team of Christians to serve Muslims in the Middle Eastern country where Steph and her family lived. John and Mary asked our team to lead the teaching and prayers during the church service while we were there. About two hundred Muslims packed the church that night. My wife and I stood in the back because every chair had been filled.

As usual, those gathered began singing Christian worship songs after the opening prayer. Elie, the Arabic Christian, led the singing. It was a very low-budget set up. The words of the worship songs appeared on a television that was placed on a high stand so everyone could see them. A laptop computer connected to the television displayed the lyrics while the songs played. Every person in there, except for a few in the front row, was standing and singing. Overwhelmed by the emotion of hearing the voices of Muslims singing Christian worship songs, my wife, Karen, and I had tears streaming down our faces.

Then Elie took the microphone and knelt next to someone sitting in the front row. Suddenly, all but one person stopped singing, and a single voice rang beautifully through the room. From the back of the room, I could not see the woman with the angelic voice.

When the song ended, everyone erupted with applause. Muslims were shouting, screaming, and leaping with abundant joy. That was the most inspirational worship my wife and I had ever experienced anywhere in the world. We were not in a Christian nation. This was not a church filled with expensive audiovisual equipment and led by a professionally trained worship leader singing with other Christians. This was an Islamic nation, and a dangerous area at that. The simple house church was led by untrained Christians who used a few hundred dollars' worth of electronic equipment and sang with Muslims. The Holy Spirit was present in a powerful way, stirring the church into a frenzy of praise. My wife and I went from silent tears to sobs of gratitude and awe of this special moment. Even now, the sweet memory brings tears to my eyes.

Steph and I

After the worship time, I worked to regain my composure so I could teach the lesson. As I walked to the front of the room, I could see the three people in the front row who had not stood during the singing. One was the young woman in a wheelchair who had sung the beautiful solo. Two women wearing veils sat beside her. It was Steph and her mother and aunt.

After sharing the gospel through the Bible, I asked if anyone was ready to accept Christ as Lord and Savior. None responded. Then I asked for those who wanted someone to pray for them in Jesus's name to seek a team member and make their requests known. Before I could finish my sentence, Steph's mom leaped out of her chair, carried Steph in her arms, and brought her to me. They had faith and believed that God would do a miracle through me that night to heal Steph. They were ready to throw away the wheelchair because Steph would no longer need it after the prayer.

My wife and I laid hands on Steph, and I prayed. I believed wholeheartedly that God would miraculously heal Steph. I prayed confidently, closed the prayer in the name of Jesus, and opened my eyes, expecting Steph to get up and walk.

The Miracle

Steph was not healed; she did not walk. Encouraged by the presence of Amir, I kept pleading with God to do a miracle with Steph as He had done with Amir. Others joined me as well in heartfelt prayers, but Steph was not physically healed.

Disappointed, perplexed, but unhindered, Steph and her family kept coming back to the house church meetings. They kept listening to, reading, and studying the Bible. They kept praying in Jesus's name, and praising God in song.

During our time in the country, my wife and I grew close to Steph and her family, and we were filled with joy each time we saw their smiling faces. They inspired us with their joy despite their extremely tough circumstances.

Karen's vacation time from her job was almost over, and she was due to fly home the upcoming Monday. We planned to end Karen's time in the Middle East with a special worship service where the small mission team would wash the feet of Muslims in attendance that Saturday night.

The house church leaders there warned us it was possible that none of the Muslims would come forward to allow any of us to wash their feet. We understood, but we also felt strongly that God wanted us to do a foot-washing service that night. We prepared for the evening with water, buckets, and towels. We also prepared for potential feelings of rejection, as we knew that it was possible that no one would come forward.

After our typical time of worship songs and Bible teaching, I invited the Muslim women first to come forward to have their feet washed by Christian women. Again, before I could finish my sentence, Steph's mom leaped out of her seat and picked Steph up out of the wheelchair. Both women simultaneously kept loudly repeating, "Karen! Karen! Karen!"

Karen came forward and gently began to wash Steph's feet. The Holy Spirit overwhelmed the room with His presence that night. Karen and Steph began crying, then sobbing, and within seconds every person in that room was crying. There was not a dry eye in the place.

Steph's mom and aunt waited in turn to have Karen wash their feet. Then other Muslims, more than forty of them—men, women, and children—lined up to have the Christians from our small team wash their feet.

Steph, her mom, and her aunt asked for special prayers that

night. For the first time in about a year of weekly prayer requests for miraculous physical healing, they did not ask for such that Saturday night. Instead, beginning with Steph, all three asked to pray to receive Jesus as Lord and Savior. Nine other Muslims prayed with us that night to accept Christ.

In total, twelve Muslims accepted Jesus that night. The youngest was a teenage boy, and the oldest was a man in his sixties. That Saturday, males and females, young and old, joined Steph (who was now twenty years old) as new believers in Christ.

The following Monday morning, Karen traveled home while I stayed two more weeks in the Middle East sharing the good news with Muslims. Karen asked me to give Steph a special hug when I was scheduled to see her later in the week.

Karen and I never saw Steph again.

Days after accepting Christ as Lord and Savior, Steph became suddenly ill and died.

The day I found out about Steph passing on was one of the saddest of my life. In my grief, I was also deeply concerned about the impact Steph's sudden and unexpected death might have on new believers, like her mom and aunt. But their response surprised me. Of course, they were sad, but they also felt special peace and joy. They explained that they had asked God for miraculous physical healing for Steph without realizing that He was already at work in their lives. They believed God already had done the impossible by protecting them as they fled raging war with Steph in a wheelchair. Somehow, they had made it through rough terrain to safely arrive at the tent city; then, among millions of Muslim refugees, God led them to discover the house church.

As they kept coming back to the church seeking an earthly, physical miracle, God had the best miracle in mind. God planted His word in them through the Bible, displayed His love for them through Christians, and opened Steph's heart and mind to see the truth about Jesus. All along the way, they said, God was using their tremendous, war-related losses to prepare their hearts for the only thing they could never lose: God's gift of eternal life through Jesus Christ.

Now, they knew, Steph had gone ahead of them into the presence of God. They were comforted by the assurance that Steph is in heaven, healed wholly and eternally. And they knew without a doubt that she would join the angels in songs of praise to God. Their spiritually mature response eased my own sadness and gave me peace and joy.

Karen and I feel blessed that God gave us the opportunity to be part of Steph's story.

When There Are No Physical Miracles

So back to the question before the above stories: *Do miracles still happen?* I believe so, but from Steph and others like her, I have learned that the miracle may not be what we expect or hope. God does not perform at our command to heal people or perform other visible miracles. As I shared earlier, I've prayed for countless physical miracles that didn't happen. I have also witnessed God doing miracles—and when He does, His spectacular display of power produces a tremendous harvest among Muslims. Even when there are no physical miracles, there are often spiritual ones, like the one with Steph and her family.

Hundreds of the Muslims with whom I have prayed have come back to me and other Christians asking for more prayers. They often report that when they prayed in the name of Jesus, they felt something indescribable stir within their hearts and minds, and they simply could not get enough. Like Steph, they kept coming back for more prayers in the name of Jesus, and many eventually believe in Christ as Lord and Savior.

Prayer is not about whether God chooses to do an external miracle or an internal one; rather, it is about displaying God's power and glory through prayer in the name of Jesus.

The Impact of Praying with Muslims

Years ago, I had the privilege to serve with and observe two faithful World Changers at work with Muslims. They both shared the gospel in Islamic areas with thousands of Muslims, beginning around the same time. I reviewed the results over a three-year period.

Despite working in areas that were geographically close within the same country, I was surprised to learn that one saw around thirty Muslims coming to faith in Christ, while the other led around four hundred to faith in the same three years.

The main difference between the two individuals was that one consistently prayed with Muslims in the name of Jesus as a method of sharing the gospel, and the other did not.

Praying in the name of Jesus is one of the most effective ways I have ever seen to lift up His name with a Muslim and to prepare the way to share the good news of Christ. It is one of the simplest, most God-centered, God-dependent, God-glorifying principles ever.

Why Prayer Is So Effective with Muslims

Muslims typically pray five times every day. But to the Muslims I have met, regardless of the Islamic denomination to which they belong, those daily prayers are a matter of duty, tradition, and worship. The daily prayers are ways to please Allah and gain his favor, especially in anticipation of how Allah will view them on Judgment Day.

I have met some Muslims who do petition God for personal prayer requests, such as for health or finances, etc. But I have yet to meet a Muslim who has proclaimed that Allah miraculously healed them or answered their personal petitions.

It is because prayer is a central focus of daily life for Muslims that they are already open and predisposed to it. When a Christian offers to pray to God on their behalf in the name of Jesus, a respected messenger of Allah whom the Quran suggests is alive with Allah today, they are likely to accept. This is especially the case when a

Muslim has an unmet need or is facing a problem or crisis; moreover, nothing in the Quran forbids such a prayer.

I used to be very hesitant to pray with a Muslim in the name of Jesus. I worried that, if God did not answer my prayer, then the Muslim might think negatively of Jesus.

Then God spoke to my heart and challenged me strongly with the following thoughts:

> I have prepared Muslims all their lives for the moment when a Christian (you) prays with them in the name of Jesus. It is then that they will see the difference between their lifetime of five prayers per day and a prayer requested in the name of Jesus. It is then that they will know that there is something uniquely different about the name of Jesus. So just do it and get out of the way, then you and the Muslim will see the power and glory of the Lord at work.

This understanding helped me realize that praying with a Muslim in the name of Jesus is all about Jesus. The pressure is not on me to achieve a miracle or in fact, do anything other than be a faithful witness to Jesus by lifting up His name in a special way through prayer. God decides when, if, and how to answer the prayer. If God does not answer the prayer, it will be because He knows best, and He is sovereign. But if He does decide to answer the prayer, then Jesus is set apart, and God gets the glory.

With that realization in mind, I hesitantly began to offer to pray with Muslims in the name of Jesus. I was pleasantly surprised to see the majority of Muslims I asked accept my offer. Through that process, God increased my faith in Him, as well as my reliance and dependence on Him. Most exciting of all, I got to witness God using prayer as a primary tool to help lead hundreds of Muslims to accepting Christ as their Lord and Savior.

I believe God has prepared Muslims (and Hindus, Buddhists, etc.)

for you to pray with them in the name of Jesus. And I am confident that your faithfulness in prayer will do as much for you as a Christian as it does for the Muslim for whom you pray in Jesus's name.

Islamic Apologetics Are Defenseless against Prayer

One of the reasons praying with Muslims in the name of Jesus is so effective is that there is no apologetics defense against it. Islamic leaders cannot prepare a Muslim for the effect of witnessing God answer a prayer in the name of Jesus—regardless of whether that answer came in the form of an external miracle or an internal one in the heart and mind.

In a matter of minutes, Kari planted a gospel seed with Dalilah just as the Christian leaders at the house church did with Amir and Steph. Islamic apologetics cannot prepare for or stop this gospel seed that has been nourished with prayer from taking root.

Praying Where It Is Dangerous

Sharing the good news about Jesus for the purpose of converting a Muslim to Christ is illegal in many Islamic countries. But I am not aware of any place where it is illegal to pray for a Muslim in the name of Jesus. Even where it is not illegal to pray with Muslims, doing so can be risky, as extremist Muslims may react with violence.

iHOPE workshop alumni Jonah and Suzi traveled to an Islamic nation where not only is the gospel illegal but there are also more Islamic extremists, with as much as 20 percent of the population fitting in this group. A minority of the population of this country are Christian, and they are consistently persecuted (sometimes severely, sometimes murdered) by the Islamic extremists. Considering these factors, it is not surprising that few Christians in this country risk sharing the gospel with Muslims.

Some of the dangerous and deadly conflicts in this Islamic nation were between Muslims who disagreed on the political solutions to solving the country's seemingly countless problems. Most of the conflicts were between the government's law enforcement or military fighting against extremist Muslims. Christians, in general, did not get involved in any of these conflicts; instead, they attempted to remain safe by keeping a low profile.

Suzi and Jonah traveled to this country at the request of a Christian group in that Islamic nation's largest city. As they met with Christians there, the couple proceeded to remind them lovingly and sensitively of God's second primary purpose for their lives: to make Him known. They encouraged the Christians to begin praying that God would reveal to them how they could take on their roles as ambassadors for Christ in that most effective way while minimizing personal risk. The local Christians wholeheartedly embraced the idea of praying intentionally, and they became faithful in doing so.

This prayer and God's clear presence in their lives emboldened some of the local Christians to go with Suzi and Jonah in small teams to pray with Muslims in the name of Jesus. Before setting out, they prayed that God would lead them to persons of peace.

The local Christians were pleasantly surprised to discover that many Muslims embraced their offer to pray with them. The majority of Muslims there live in financial poverty and poor healthcare, so many prayer requests focused on these issues. That Islamic nation is also continually engulfed in political turmoil that threatens to spiral out of control into military conflict, so other prayer requests revolved around people's fears and worry over the situation.

One day, while the Christians were gathering for their usual worship service, angry Islamic crowds gathered nearby for protests. The protests quickly turned violent, and chaos erupted as the crowds began fighting each other and the government forces sent to police the situation.

The Christians saw that Muslims on both sides were getting beaten, stabbed, and shot. Rather than attempting to keep a low profile, they felt compelled to do something to help the injured. They ran out of their safe meeting place and into the violence and grabbed the injured and took them into their church to mend their wounds. After addressing the immediate physical needs, the Christians began offering to pray for Muslims in the name of Jesus. The Muslims in their care accepted the offer, and some were healed miraculously.

After the riotous crowds dispersed, news spread among Muslims of the miraculous healings due to prayers in the name of Jesus. Some Muslims began to seek Christians to pray for them in the name of Jesus. The prayers led to some Muslims accepting Bibles from the Christians, asking to study the Bible with Christians, and some even accepting Jesus as Lord and Savior.

The news of these results spread among the Christian minority throughout this Islamic nation. Although the reports of Muslims becoming followers of Jesus were encouraging, many Christians remained too fearful to fulfill God's calling to be ambassadors for Christ in that nation; still, there are some Christians who have courageously embraced their role and began sharing the good news with Muslims—and they started by offering prayer in the name of Jesus.

I cannot yet report a big movement among Muslims toward Christ in that Islamic nation. I also do not know the level of impact that the spark that began with Suzi and Jonah is having on that nation. I can, however, report that these Christians are now, for the first time ever, fulfilling God's second primary purpose for their lives and that former Muslims are becoming multiplying disciples for Jesus and starting church groups of their own.

The Most Fruitful Gospel Prayer!

I have personally asked over seventeen hundred Muslims if they would pray with me to accept Jesus as their personal Lord and Savior. I always did that only when I thought it was appropriate to do so and after praying for God's guidance in the situation. Over sixty of the seventeen hundred Muslims (less than 4 percent) *initially* accepted Christ and prayed with me to receive Him as Lord and Savior.

I asked the remaining 96 percent, or around 1,640 Muslims, if they would accept a different prayer from me. I asked, "Will you pray with me to ask the Holy Spirit of God to reveal the truth to you about the identity of Jesus Christ and whether the Bible is the true and accurate word of God?" Many of these Muslims responded positively to that question. Then I prayed the following prayer with them:

> Holy God, we pray right now that Your Holy Spirit will come into the heart, mind, and soul of (insert name) to reveal the truth about the identity of Jesus Christ. Please reveal to (insert name) whether Jesus is the Messiah, the Son of God, the only Lord and Savior through whom Your free gift of salvation is available or whether Jesus was merely a human messenger. Holy God, we also pray that Your Holy Spirit will fill (insert name) and reveal to him or her whether the Bible is Your true and accurate word where you reveal Your plan of salvation.

Then I ask the Muslim to close the prayer by saying amen to God if they agree with the words of the prayer. Most do.

This prayer gets the least resistance from any Muslim I have ever encountered, including suspected Islamic extremists. Following this prayer and continued Bible study, another thousand-plus of these same 1,640 Muslims ended up accepting Jesus as Lord and Savior.

Reasons for the Effectiveness of This Prayer

Some iHOPE workshop alumni have reported similar responses and results when they've offered this prayer with Muslims. What's interesting is that, because Muslims do not believe in the Trinity, the Father, Son, and Holy Spirit, Christianity's Triune God, if we refer to the Holy Spirit as one of the Trinity, they would be opposed to the prayer. Meanwhile, Muslims do believe that God has a Spirit, and of course the Spirit is holy, so they typically and wholeheartedly agree to have the Holy Spirit of God fill them, guide them, and reveal the truth to them.

God knows the heart of every person—Christian, Muslim, or otherwise. When you pray with a potential Muslim person of peace who is sincerely seeking the truth from God about the true identity of Jesus and the truthfulness of the Bible as the word of God, God honors this prayer request.

A Muslim has a lot to lose in this life, even his or her own life, should they decide to leave Islam and become followers of Jesus. So when we pray with a Muslim to make a decision for Christ, it is profoundly serious and difficult. The above prayer invites God to reveal Jesus as Lord and for His Holy Spirit to guide the Muslim into the correct decision.

Just as praying in the name of Jesus lifts Him up in a unique way with a Muslim, so does praying that the Holy Spirit fills a Muslim to reveal the truth. Many Muslims told me they felt something stir within them after this prayer. Most of the Muslims with whom I prayed this prayer eventually accepted Jesus as Lord and Savior. So this prayer served as a seed for the truth of the Trinity, but without any theological debates or complicated conversations about the true identity or the deity of the Holy Spirit.

The Greatest Seed Nutrient Ever

When you offer a Muslim the prayer as soon as is appropriate or possible, you are taking a big step to finding a Muslim person of peace—a person whose heart (soil) God has prepared to receive the gospel seed. If a Muslim does not want your prayers in the name of Jesus, then realize that he or she may not yet be the person of peace God is leading you to meet.

In many cases, prayer can be a wonderful way to plant the gospel seed. But in all cases, it is the greatest nutrient for helping the gospel seed take root and grow. Just as it is better to let God speak for and defend His word by sharing scriptures (rather than arguments and evidence) with Muslims, when we pray in Jesus's name, we are completely relying on God to do the work of drawing people to Himself. From a strategic perspective, one of the easiest and most fruitful things you can do with a Muslim is to offer to pray in the name of Jesus. Then trust almighty God to produce the harvest.

CHAPTER 11

The Fifth Essential: Love

We have covered four of the five essentials every Christian must know and do to share Christ with Muslims and to help change the world. We know the only eternal life-giving seed to sow with Muslims, we discovered which Muslims to sow into, we learned the most fruitful seed ever, and we uncovered the most fruitful seed nutrient ever.

Is there a special planting method proven to penetrate a Muslim's heart and grow into a most fruitful harvest?

Yes!

God calls this seed-planting way the greatest and the best. God states that without it, the other four essentials are like nothing. Without this fifth essential, it is unlikely that we will see a harvest at all, but with it the fields become ready for harvest (see John 4:35). Islamic apologists cannot defend against it, it is legal everywhere, and it's universally accepted and even embraced. The following story illustrates this fifth essential: *love.*

Muslim Seeks to Convert Christians

Mustafa moved to a Christianized nation to attend college. He was a devout Muslim from a close-knit family in an Islamic nation where the gospel and conversion to Christianity is illegal and punishable by death. Mustafa memorized the Quran and was extremely knowledgeable in all other holy Islamic teachings and texts. He also prepared for moving into a Christianized country by training in Islamic apologetics.

Mustafa knew of Christians in his Islamic country, but none had ever engaged him with any spiritual conversations, and he had never heard the good news about Jesus. Mustafa thought Christians were well-meaning but ignorant of God's truth. A brilliant debater with excellent reasoning skills, he was looking forward to using his knowledge and skills to convert the Christians he would meet into Muslims.

A Christian Host

Debi and Stan were hard-working Christians with a desire to fulfill God's purpose by spreading the gospel. Their middle-class family earned just enough money to live. They didn't have much money to put in the collection plate at church, but they did have an extra bedroom in their home, and they felt led by God to use that room to host an international student from the local university.

The student organization that partnered with the university to serve international students assigned Mustafa to their home. Stan and Debi did not know much about Islamic culture, Islam, the Quran, or any of Islam's holy literature or teachings. They did not think they could adequately answer the theological questions a Muslim student may have, but they were willing to be the best Christian hosts possible.

Debi and Stan's Approach

Just as he planned and prepared for, Mustafa brought up tough theological issues and questions with Stan and Debi, hoping to lead them into Islam. And just as they anticipated, Stan and Debi felt ill-equipped to answer Mustafa's questions. They responded with heartfelt sincerity and a typical two-fold response: "That's a great question, Mustafa. We're not sure that we can give you an adequate answer, so we'll pray right now that God will provide you with the correct answer. 'God, please speak into Mustafa's heart and reveal Your answer. In Jesus's name, amen.'"

Debi and Stan would then proceed by saying something like this to Mustafa: "Please forgive us for not knowing the answers you seek. But please know that Jesus put God's love for you in our heart. In the Bible, God tells us 'Let us love one another, for love is from God.' Mustafa, we love you!"

Even when Stan and Debi thought they knew an accurate response to Mustafa, they were too hesitant to give it. They were afraid that they did not know enough about Islamic culture or Islam and that their response may be offensive to Mustafa. To avoid making cultural blunders, they decided to keep responding with prayer and by showing him the sincere love they felt for him using both their words and actions.

Over time, Debi and Stan felt more confident that responding to Mustafa with God's love was the right approach. Whenever they thought it appropriate, they added a different verse to their response to emphasize God's love. One verse at a time, they shared God's word from sections such as 1 John 4:7–21; John 13:34–35; 1 Corinthians 13; Matthew 22:37–39; etc.

Debi and Stan continued showing love to Mustafa in this way for the four years he lived with them; meanwhile, Mustafa began to feel love toward them and respected them immensely. Mustafa also concluded that he could not persuade Stan and Debi to become Muslims, so he offered them a Quran, which they accepted. Mustafa also began to pray intentionally that Allah would lead them to be Muslims and usher them into paradise.

It was a bittersweet day after Mustafa graduated and was moving out from Debi and Stan's home. Emboldened by Mustafa's gift to them, Debi and Stan offered a study Bible to Mustafa as a graduation and parting gift. They were thrilled when Mustafa accepted their gift.

A Lasting Impression

Mustafa got a job in the Christianized nation that would train him for a permanent position back in his Islamic home country. After moving out of Stan and Debi's home, Mustafa began to realize the tremendous impact their love had had on him personally. He found himself pondering their loving actions and words constantly. Mustafa had never experienced that kind of love; he thought it was divine.

Then Mustafa began to recall some of the love quotes Debi and Stan had shared from the Bible. Mustafa never imagined he would ever be interested in reading a Bible, a book he thought had been corrupted by Christians. But the unique love he witnessed from Debi and Stan compelled him to read the Bible. He wanted to understand what was in the Bible that would lead Debi and Stan to love like that.

Mustafa began a three-year journey of studying the Bible on his own, ending with Mustafa accepting Jesus Christ as his Lord and Savior. Mustafa shares that it was the love of Christ flowing through Debi and Stan that propelled him into that eternal-life changing journey.

The Most Excellent Way

If you haven't already guessed, the fifth essential every Christian must know and do with Muslims is to love them as God loves them. Love them in thoughts, words, and actions.

A common thread in the thousands of testimonies I've read and heard from former Muslims is the tremendous impact of the love of Christ flowing to them through a Christian. In every story I have shared with you so far, the love of God for the Muslim was on display through the Christian who interacted with, prayed with, studied with, and/or gave a Bible to a Muslim. Loving a Muslim person of peace through a personal relationship is the greatest gospel seed-planting way ever!

First Corinthians 12:31–13:13, depending on the translation, calls love the "most excellent" way, the "greatest" way, and "a way of life that is best of all." These two chapters explain that it is possible to use all your other gifts and talents (and even the other four essentials) to share the gospel with Muslims, but if you do not do it with love, then it is like doing nothing. In contrast, when God's love shines through you, the five essentials become incredibly effective and produce a fruitful harvest.

God Enables and Perfects Love in Us

Many Christians come to the iHOPE workshops to learn about what they should "do about" Muslims. They want a solution, but when they find out that the solution requires that they respond to Jesus's command to share the gospel—with Muslims—they feel both equipped and concerned. I've had many come to me with questions about how to change their hearts toward Muslims. They may say something like, "Now I know we need to share the gospel with Muslims, and you have taught us how to do it effectively. But I don't love Muslims. Is it possible that I can grow to love them? And if so, how?"

The Bible answers these important and relevant questions, so let us briefly review some passages together. We will begin with a passage Debi and Stan shared with Mustafa. The passage is in 1 John 4:7–5:5. The following are a few highlights from the New Living Translation:

> Love comes from God ... But anyone who does not love does not know God, for God is love ... No one has ever seen God. But if we love each other, God lives in us, and his love is brought to full expression in us ... God is love, and all who live in love live in God, and God lives in them. And as we live in God, our love grows more perfect. So we will not be afraid on the day of judgment, but we can face him with confidence because we live like Jesus here in this world.

I used to hate Muslims, and it took years after I accepted Jesus as my Lord and Savior for that to change. Based on the Bible passage you just read, and within the context of the rest of the Bible, you and I are not capable of loving others God's way. Rather, we begin the process of loving others as a result of accepting Christ.

According to verse 7, we love because we have been "born of God" (NIV) and as such are children of God (NLT). According to verse 13 in both the NIV and NLT, it is in love that God gives us His Spirit, and He lives in us. It is God's presence in us that enables us to love others, including Muslims, in God's way.

Loving others begins a process that verses 17–18 refer to as love being "made complete" in us and of us being "made perfect in love" (NIV). The NLT puts it this way: "Our love grows more perfect." When we can love without fear, we "experience His perfect love." As we grow as God's children, God perfects His love in us and makes us more complete. In my own heart and life, as is true for every Christian, the Spirit of God removed my hate for Muslims and replaced it with His love.

When Christians become aware of their lack of love or of their anger, hatred, or indifference toward Muslims, they also become aware of the real Islamic problem: the Muslim's desperate need for Jesus *and* the need for Christians to share Jesus with Muslims. As we bring the problem within our hearts to God, the Holy Spirit begins the transformation process and fills us with God's love. In my own life, this process took me from hating God to loving Him wholeheartedly. His Holy Spirit and love then filled me with His love in such a way that I could not help but love Muslims (and others) because God, who is love, loves them.

True Love Is ...

This passage also teaches, as does the entire Bible, that God's love is not merely a feeling or sentiment. Verse 9 tells us that God revealed His love for us through action: "God showed how much he loved us by sending his one and only Son into the world so that we might have eternal life through him" (NLT).

God initiated the action that made salvation possible to a lost world, and much of the world is ignorant of its need of Him. In response to God's love, His children—Christians—ought to initiate loving action and tell the 1.43 billion Muslims of the good news of Jesus. In love, we must tell Muslims that Jesus is the only way to be reconciled to God.

God's Two Primary Purposes Reinforced

These verses in 1 John also reinforce God's two primary purposes for His children. First, we must know God, which means we grow to love Him through a close, personal relationship. Second, we are to love others, including Muslims, as He loves us. In so doing, we help others know Him.

This passage also reinforces the message Jesus shared in John 15: Love comes not from our own power, but from Him. In other words, He empowers us with His love to accomplish His two primary purposes for our lives. In 1 John 4:15–16 the English Standard Version puts it this way: "God abides in him, and he in God ... whoever abides in love abides in God, and God abides in him."

Jesus talks about the same thing in John 15. There you see the same interconnected two points: Abide in God. Your connection to Him is manifested when you love others, which results in being fruitful and multiplying.

Only after I abided in God and He in me did He transform my heart from hating to loving Muslims. That transformation—which God brought about—allowed and still allows Him to use me to make Himself known to Muslims and to reconcile them to Himself through Jesus.

Why Love Works So Well

Science tell us—and human history and experience confirm—that love is a fundamental human need. God wired us to need love from inception in the womb until death. The greatest love we can ever experience is God's love. Since the beginning of time, however, humans have tried to get love from everywhere other than the only source of true love. We thirst and hunger for love, and we try to fill our need with something other than God ... and it never works. The world can never satisfy the need we have to experience God's love.

Muslims share this common and fundamental human need for love. They, too, are trying to fill their need for love with things other than the God of the Bible—the God who *is* love; therefore, they are not satisfied, and they do not know what they are missing. If you equate love to a physical or nutritional need, substituting anything else for God's love is like trying to meet the body's nutritional needs with a diet of pure sugar. The body will never be satisfied—yet may not know what it was missing—until nutrient-rich foods are introduced into the diet; likewise, it is only when Muslims get to know the God of the Bible who offers love and eternal reconciliation through the gift of Jesus that they can experience the His love firsthand.

When you as a Christian connect with a Muslim person of peace, the love of Jesus can flow through you to that Muslim. That is exactly what happened with Debi and Stan connecting with Mustafa. He recognized that there was something different about their love; it was deeper and sincerer than any other love Mustafa had ever experienced. The reason? Mustafa was feeling and witnessing the love of the God for the very first time in his life. All the Islamic apologetics Mustafa had learned did not meet his need for the love of Christ. When he was the recipient of the love of Jesus through Debi and Stan, God began to satisfy that fundamental human need for love. Mustafa did not initially comprehend what was happening to him; he just knew it was internally satisfying and that he wanted and needed more of it.

God's love is too attractive and irresistible to the person of peace.

When you actively show and share God's love with others, you are using one of the wisest and most effective strategies for spreading the gospel.

Loving Where It Is Dangerous

Angie is an English teacher in a Christianized nation. She wanted to use her God-given gifts to be fruitful and multiply, so she began teaching English at a refugee center in her city. Most of the refugees there were Muslims from Islamic countries. Angie knew very little about Islam, Islamic culture, or Muslims in general, and she was eager to learn from her students.

It typically took at least six months of English study before she and her students could have long or in-depth conversations. But even when words failed her, Angie communicated her love for them in so many nonverbal ways. Angie's students felt her deep and sincere love for them. When they were finally able to converse in English, her students felt amazingly comfortable talking about spiritual matters with her. Some of Angie's students became believers in Jesus as their Lord and Savior, and they credited her love as the key that opened the door to wanting to know more about Him.

Sabah was one of Angie's students who became a Christian. Sabah was a Muslim refugee who came from an Islamic nation with various warring factions. Angie loved Sabah like a sister, and they got close even though verbal communication was initially difficult due to the language barrier. Through Angie's computer, Sabah communicated via video calls with her brother Rafi, who still lived in the Islamic country. After she became a Christian, Sabah shared the good news about Jesus with Rafi. He tried—and failed—to persuade his younger sister away from Christianity and back to Islam; instead, after months of video calls with Sabah and Angie, Rafi accepted Jesus as his Lord and Savior.

Rafi, Sabah, and Angie continued to have ongoing Bible studies via video calls. Rafi then brought a close Muslim friend with him to the Bible study, and then another, and then another. After a few months, Rafi shared that some of his Muslim friends appeared ready to accept Jesus but were afraid of persecution. Rafi asked if Angie and her husband would be willing to travel to his Islamic country, believing their personal presence would make a significant impact.

Angie, accompanied by three others, traveled there to visit with Rafi and the Muslim seekers within his circle of influence. During the two weeks Angie and the Christian team were there, nine Muslims accepted Jesus. They all stated that the love Angie and the team displayed by simply risking so much to be there impressed upon them that the God of the Bible must be the true God.

Filled with God's love, they began to share the gospel with others. Within two years, they had established house churches throughout the city where around two hundred Christians from Muslim backgrounds met to worship. One of the new Christians was a son of a powerful Islamic extremist leader. Once the leader discovered his son's conversion, he began to persecute the church. He would identify Christians, apprehend them, and offer them the ultimatum to either convert back to Islam or die. Within months, about one hundred of the two hundred were killed for conversion and blasphemy. The underground church stopped sharing the good news and ceased Bible studies with Muslim seekers.

Rafi told Angie they would need her to visit their country and city once again to help restart the movement. After a period of fasting and praying, Angie and her husband agreed that she would go back for a short visit. They knew the dangers, so this time they decided Angie would go alone, without a team, so no one else would be in danger.

Back in the city, Angie, Rafi, and the remaining Christians from Muslim background prayed, worshiped, and mourned together for their extensive losses. Angie spent several days doing that through the remaining house churches. Rafi and the leaders organized one large meeting at a location that could fit the one hundred remaining Christians. They asked Angie to sit in the front, visible to everyone. Then Rafi read a letter signed by every single one of them.

In summary, they thanked Angie for displaying how much she and her family loved them that she was willing to risk her life with them against the threat of the Islamic extremist leader. The risk she took in going there also revealed Angie's love for the God of the Bible, that she was willing to risk her life for the sake of Jesus. Angie's sacrificial love motivated them to restart sharing the gospel and resuming Bible studies once again.

Angie got back home safely, while Rafi and the Christians continued to face deadly persecution. Despite the threats on their lives, God was clearly at work. An incredible number of Muslims accepted Jesus as Lord and Savior. The sacrificial love Angie, Rafi, and the rest of the former Muslims had displayed by risking their lives for the sake of the gospel helped fuel the increase.

This movement began with the love of Christ flowing through Angie as she used her God-given gifts with Muslims. Angie is an average Christian, not a theologian or a pastor. She was not educated about Islam, its people, or its politics. She simply became a channel for God's love to Muslims. I pray you will also help change the world by becoming a channel for the love of Christ.

Love Where the Gospel Is Illegal

Melissa and Ken are a married couple from a Christianized nation. With tremendous emotional difficulty, they left their families and beloved nation, answering God's call to move to an Islamic country. Sharing the gospel or making any attempt to convert a Muslim to Christianity was illegal in their new country. The nation was experiencing significant political conflict, and Islamic extremism was on the rise. Between the political tension and the terrorism, the unstable country was in turmoil.

Many people in that Islamic country believe that better education is a key to solving its many problems. Learning the English language plays a vital role in that education and in improving the country's economic opportunities. These needs opened the doors for Melissa and Ken to get jobs at a university teaching English as a foreign language. They were not teachers before going to this country, but by taking a three-month course and earning a certification, they learned it is possible to get jobs teaching English in many Islamic countries.

Inayah was one of their college students and came from a large, devout Muslim family. Inayah had heard of Christianity before but only knew it as one of the false religions of the world. Inayah did not know what to expect of Christians but thought they would be bad and untrustworthy. She was surprised when Melissa and Ken made an unexpected positive impression on her. Immediately, she wanted to know them better. A friendship between them formed, and they began a weekly tradition of Melissa and Ken preparing a dinner from their home country and Inayah teaching them to cook some of her own favorite meals.

Their Love Was Different

Inayah noticed the close, mutually respectful, loving relationship between Melissa and Ken. Little things made a big impact on her—for example, Ken and Melissa holding hands and praying before each meal. And things like Ken cleaning up after dinner, while Melissa and Inayah enjoyed each other's company. She also noticed the loving way Ken and Melissa glanced at each other. She realized how different Melissa and Ken's love was compared to what she had witnessed all her life with her parents and other Muslim couples. Inayah began to pray that God would put her in a mutually loving relationship like the one Ken and Melissa shared.

Melissa and Ken grew to love Inayah as their little sister. Inayah felt loved by them in a way that was deeper and more genuine than she had ever felt before. Initially, Inayah could not describe it, but she enjoyed it very much and wanted more.

Inayah became inspired to become a teacher like Melissa and Ken. But she discovered that the wages of a teacher in her country, even English ones like Ken and Melissa, were low, even more so for a female. Inayah then began researching wages for teachers in other nations, including the Christianized nation where Melissa and Ken came from. To her surprise, Inayah found that wages were much higher there.

As Inayah became more comfortable with Melissa and Ken, she asked, "Why would you come from a safer and wealthier Christian country, where you can both earn more money, to come here where it is risky and dangerous?"

Melissa and Ken had been long ready for such a question and answered, "Because Jesus loves Muslims in this country, but they do not know about Him or His love for them. Jesus put His love for Muslims in our hearts and inspired us to come here to help Muslims by teaching them English and sharing His love with them. In the Bible, Jesus tells us (Acts 1:8) that we are to be His witnesses, telling people about Him everywhere."

"How Do I Find Out More?"

Inayah knew in her heart there was something incredibly special about Jesus and His love; how else could she explain what had inspired Melissa and Ken to love like that? Curious, Inayah asked them how she could learn and know more about Jesus and His love. Thrilled with her interest, they showed Inayah how to get an online study Bible app, and she did.

Studying the Bible to learn more about Jesus became Inayah's favorite thing to do. Within a year, Inayah believed in Jesus Christ as her Lord and Savior. But Inayah kept that a secret from everyone except for Melissa and Ken. Inayah feared what would happen with her parents, especially her father.

Zealot Islamic Student

Ken and Melissa had another student in a different class at the university: Abad. Like Inayah, Abad came from a large, devout Muslim family. And like her, Abad had similar perceptions about Christianity and Christians. Ken and Melissa were the first Christians Abad had ever met.

Abad possessed excellent leadership qualities. His parents hoped he would grow to become an influential Islamic leader, so they invested much time and effort to groom him as such. Abad blossomed and became extremely knowledgeable in Islamic holy books. Students in the university, as well as many Muslims in the city, recognized and followed Abad as a young leader with growing influence.

But like Inayah, Abad was also amazed at Ken and Melissa's love. Abad eventually asked them a question like Inayah's, and Ken and Melissa gave the same response about making Jesus and His love for Muslims known. Their love compelled Abad into learning more about Jesus, and he, too, began studying the Bible. It took Abad two years of praying and studying the Bible to reach the point of accepting Jesus as his Lord and Savior. After making that decision, he was faced with fears similar to Inayah's about the response of his family. Through Ken and Melissa, Abad connected with other new Christians from Muslim backgrounds who dealt with similar obstacles, and they all formed networks of support groups. Then they began the difficult and risky process of informing their families of their new Christian faith.

Persecution followed often, but it seemed to fuel the growth of the number of believers. Inayah and Abad met through one of these groups, fell in love, and got married. They are raising their children as Christians and continue today to risk sharing the good news of Jesus Christ as Lord and Savior. They are recognized as leaders in the movement of multiplying disciples of Jesus.

Most of the believers in this dangerous Islamic nation credit the love of Christ flowing through Melissa and Ken as the spark that propelled them into the eternal life–changing journey. God wants to do the same through you.

CHAPTER 12
Four Next Steps

We have uncovered the root of the problem that has turned the Middle East and North Africa (MENA) from being the place where Christianity was born and was Christianized to now being almost all Muslim. We have seen how the root problem affects today's Christianized nations, with trends indicating that it is not a matter of if but *when* what has already happened in MENA will occur in your nation.

Those trends will continue—unless we become part of the solution. As we have explored the five essentials every Christian must know and do with Muslims, I hope you have come to understand not only the need but also how simple, doable, and duplicable these five essentials are. For quick reference, here are the five essentials:

1. Share the gospel. Be mindful that God has called you to be fruitful and multiply. His two main purposes for your life are to know Him and to make Him known.
2. Seek out a person of peace. Your responsibility is to rely on God. At no point are you in this alone. Ask the Holy Spirit to guide you to the Muslim whose heart He has prepared to receive the gospel seed.
3. Give the Muslim a Bible as soon as it is possible and appropriate to do so; then, be available and willing to study the Bible with him or her and to answer questions. Rely on the Bible—God's word—to be its own defense.

4. Pray with Muslims in the name of Jesus as soon as it is appropriate to do so. Praying with people can be a way to lift up the name of Jesus and to glorify God. God may or may not see fit to do an external miracle in that person's life, but He is always ready to answer the requests of sincere seekers who want to know Him and discover the truth about Jesus.
5. Love Muslims the way God loves Muslims. Take action by showing and sharing the love God has given you.

Unfortunately, the majority of Christians are unknowingly contributing to the problem by not doing these timeless biblical principles. The story in this concluding chapter will show you potential next steps and actionable ideas you can do to live out God's primary purposes for your life. In doing so, you can help change the world, making a better future for the generations to come.

The following story will help you discover specific roles as an individual that may be well suited for the gifts, talents, and resources God has given you. It will also give you ideas that may be a fit for your organization or church. The story also highlights God's primary purposes for the life of every human being—the two we have already discussed as well as a third that is essential for you to know and understand.

The Muslims Are Coming

Roger is a Christian who was born and raised in a Christianized nation. He enjoys his office job in a corporation where he has a stellar reputation as a faithful worker and a godly person. Roger lives in a city where the Muslim population is growing due to both immigration and conversion to Islam. Roger regularly attends his local church and takes part in a weekly Bible study.

During Roger's lifetime, the section of the nation where he lives went from not having any Muslims to having hundreds of thousands. When he was growing up, there were no mosques in his surrounding area; now there are hundreds. Within a two-year period, three mosques opened (close to his church) to serve the growing Muslim population in that neighborhood.

Roger was concerned about the anger and fear some Christians at his church communicated regarding Muslims in the area. He was also saddened to learn about anti-Muslim protests and attacks on Muslim prayer gatherings. The most concerning event occurred when local citizens gathered around a mosque and protested the presence of new mosques in their neighborhoods while legally carrying weapons and banners that displayed anti-Muslim messages.

Roger's church hosted some trainings regarding Islam, Muslims, and their cultures. The trainings were led by "experts" who followed the practices of the least effective majority. Not surprisingly, the trainings failed to resonate with the audience or generate the desired outcome of inspiring congregants to create gospel-centered connections with Muslims. Most of the people in attendance, including Roger, felt overwhelmed by the complicated methodologies these experts presented. They left feeling that, to be effective, they would need knowledge about Islam, its holy books, and Muslim cultures. Even Roger, who had a heart to minister to Muslims, felt disempowered to do so.

Then Roger's work colleague recommended he attend iHOPE Ministries' workshops that were coming to a nearby city. Roger attended the workshops and discovered the five essentials. The workshops resonated with Roger and empowered him to believe that he could, in fact, do the five essentials; moreover, for the first time, Roger became aware of the root problem in his city and country and felt he could be part of the solution.

After the workshops, he began contributing a small amount from his limited income every month to iHOPE Ministries so that more Christians could be empowered to reach Muslims. But he wanted to do more than give money, so he became part of iHOPE's monthly prayer team, called iPray. The iHOPE iPray team prays for specific things related to iHOPE Ministries, for the salvation of Muslims and for the individuals who are in gospel-centered relationships with Muslims both locally and globally.) Still, he wanted to do more than to pray and give.

Response of the Church

Roger had experienced the distinct difference between iHOPE training content and the Muslim outreach training he had attended through his church. Roger believed the iHOPE workshops were exactly what his church needed, so he became an iHOPE advocate to his church. Understandably, Roger's church leaders were reluctant to host yet another workshop related to Muslim outreach. They didn't know how different and empowering the five essentials were in comparison to the robust, complex Muslim outreach training they'd just offered. After the church leaders understood some of the differences, and after prayerful consideration, Roger's church became eager to host iHOPE workshops.

The church leadership promoted the iHOPE workshops with their members and asked their members to invite people within their circles of influence. They also invited neighboring churches to attend iHOPE workshops. Hundreds of people showed up from dozens of churches in the area to attend the workshops.

Response of the Leadership

The church leadership team was inspired by what they learned and felt inspired to take action to model the five essentials with their congregants as well as with their neighboring churches and their city at large. Some put the five essentials into practice as they reached out to Muslim refugees in their city; others sought out Muslim international students or Muslims they met in and around town.

Response of the Congregants

The iHOPE workshops also resonated with the church congregants. Roger and other church members were inspired to follow their leaders' examples. They invited Muslims to their church's worship services and developed friendships with their Muslim coworkers and neighbors. A few started small Bible study groups for Muslim seekers, and through the prayer and the power of God's word, several Muslims accepted Jesus and were baptized and discipled.

Some members of the church also prayed for, donated to, and used their unique gifts to serve alongside iHOPE Ministries so that other believers could be inspired to be part of the solution to Christianity's Islamic problem.

Making a Global Impact

In addition to reaching out to Muslims locally, Roger wanted to reach Muslims globally as an online English language partner. So we connected him to some Christian evangelistic partners in a Muslim country overseas. Roger's first student was Abdallah, and he knew just enough English to hold a basic conversation. After their first video call together, Roger called me in a panic. Abdallah had informed Roger that he was the son of a top militant leader in an organization labeled as a terrorist group by Western nations. Roger wondered whether to continue conversations with Abdallah.

After we talked and prayed about the situation, Roger believed that Abdallah was indeed a Muslim person of peace, and he decided to continue with their conversations. Abdallah accepted prayers in the name of Jesus from Roger and studied the Bible with him.

Son of a Terrorist Turns Christian

After a few months of weekly conversations, Roger felt prompted in his spirit to ask Abdallah about who he thought Jesus was: a messenger, or God the Son?

On that call, Abdallah accepted Jesus as his Lord and Savior. But because of a bit of a language barrier, Roger was not sure if he understood the situation clearly or whether Abdallah had truly accepted Jesus. So I joined their next video call and asked Abdallah in Arabic about the situation. In response, Abdallah opened his Bible to Romans 10:9 (NIV) and read it: "If you declare with your mouth, 'Jesus is Lord,' and believe in your heart that God raised him from the dead, you will be saved."

Abdallah went on to explain the gospel as he understood it, and he articulated it well and accurately. Roger and I closed our call with Abdallah by asking him about any prayer requests he had. Abdallah thought about it briefly and then responded, "I pray that there are more Christians like Roger and you that love Muslims enough to take time to befriend them and share the good news of Jesus with them."

As of the writing of this book, I have a bittersweet ending for Abdallah's story. For a few months after accepting Jesus, Abdallah was engaged in a discipleship Bible study that our partners do with new Christians from Muslim backgrounds.

Then Abdallah disappeared.

Our partners believe Abdallah was perhaps taken by his father once he discovered he had become a Christian. They think Abdallah's father either killed him for not going back to Islam, or that he might still be holding Abdallah as prisoner, hoping to eventually turn him back to Islam.

Regardless, Roger and I are extremely saddened by the disappearance of Abdallah. And yet we know that Abdallah's faith in Jesus was real and that he was passionate as a disciple. Our on-the-ground Christian partners have reaffirmed that he knew the risks associated with his conversion, and Abdallah knew eternal life with

Jesus was worth the earthly risks. Abdullah has eternal life, and we are all pleased that Abdallah became a follower of Jesus before his disappearance. Meanwhile, we pray for Abdallah's immediate safe return.

The Short-Term Trip

Roger continued as an online English conversation partner, and he got to know more Muslims like Abdallah. He also encouraged and prayed with the Christian team discipling Muslims in-country. These connections and the results he saw made Roger want to visit the Islamic country; meanwhile, a few others who had attended the iHOPE workshop at his church also became global online English language partners. Not long afterward, several of them told us that they, too, wanted to visit the Muslims they had met online, as well as the Christian team discipling them locally.

Partnering with iHOPE, their church, and our evangelistic partners in the Islamic country, we worked out details and planned a trip to the Middle East. Before iHOPE made the final selection of the individuals who would be part of the team, we fasted and prayed with all the family members of those who wanted to go. Roger's wife understood the potential risks to her husband for such a trip. Believing that the safest place Roger could be is exactly where God wanted him to be, his wife gave her blessing for the trip.

Childlike Excitement

The small team arrived in the Islamic nation safely. The next day we boarded the vehicle for the one-hour ride to the city where one of our evangelistic partners operate. It was so much fun watching Roger, a grown man, display so much giddiness and childlike excitement about meeting in person the Muslims with whom he had been conversing with the prior year. The closer we got, the more excited each team member became.

As soon as the vehicle stopped, Roger leaped out and looked for the face of his Muslim friend Fadi through a sea of people on the crowded city street. Then we heard a voice shout with a heavy accent, "Roger!" Roger saw Fadi and shouted back his name. It was so emotionally moving and precious for all of us as we saw two grown men, one Christian and one Muslim, from different sides of the earth, sprint toward each other.

They embraced. Overwhelmed by emotions, they both began to cry. Then Fadi gave an ethnic greeting to Roger. Fadi grabbed Roger's head with both of his hands and began kissing him on both cheeks. Roger said that was the first time another man had ever kissed him. Roger warmed up to the idea, went out of his comfort zone, and kissed Fadi's cheeks as well.

The people on the street slowed down and took notice of Roger and Fadi's warm greeting. They realized that Roger was a foreigner, taller than most of them, with noticeably light skin and hair color, and that Fadi was clearly thrilled to see him. Some wonderful seeds for cross-cultural friendships were sown that day on that street of that Islamic city.

New Believers from Muslim Backgrounds

During the ten days our small team of Christians was there, we worked in collaboration with a few evangelistic partners in that Islamic area. The team gave hundreds of Bibles to Muslims in print and audio formats, shared the gospel, did Bible studies, and prayed in Jesus's name with hundreds of Muslim persons of peace. Many Muslims commented about how they were deeply touched by the love displayed from our team toward them. We knew it was the love of Christ flowing through us.

The team was blessed to help lead dozens of these Muslims to Jesus as Lord and Savior. One of them was Roger leading Fadi to Christ, a wonderful blessing for all of us to witness. Later these new believers were discipled by the on-the-ground Christian teams. And

Roger and the other team members continued with their English language conversations long after returning home.

Terrorist Attack

Isabella, a college student, was one of the people who attended the iHOPE workshops at Roger's church. Isabella went overseas for several weeks to serve with iHOPE evangelistic partners in an Islamic area. One of the ways Isabella ministered there was to go to poor Islamic areas and help with children's programs. One day during the trip, Isabella partnered with another female Christian, Ava, to visit the children in that poor area. (Ava was also from a Christianized nation but had moved to the country long term because she wanted to share the good news of Jesus with Muslims there.) That morning I got a text from Isabella asking for urgent prayer. An Islamic terrorist attack had struck near to where she was. The place shook with a loud explosion, as if a violent earthquake had rocked the land. The military quickly cut off the area where Isabella was, so no one was allowed in or out. I called Isabella, but she did not answer her phone.

I love Isabella like a daughter and was overwhelmed with concern for her safety. I felt helpless. But there was something I could do, so I did: I got on my knees and pleaded with God for Isabella and Ava's safety and then contacted the iHOPE prayer team so they could pray for them as well.

The next hour felt like an eternity as we waited and prayed to hear from Isabella. I then got a text from her: "We're all okay. Please keep praying. I can't believe the awesome things God is doing right now. I'll contact you when I can."

It took a couple of awfully long hours before I heard from Isabella again. I was thrilled to hear from her and to learn how God was working. Our evangelistic partners there had been ministering to Muslims in the area for years. They loved them, shared the gospel, did Bible studies, and prayed in the name of Jesus with them. The nearby terrorist attack was the tipping point that thrust some of them, both individuals and families, into accepting Jesus as their Lord and Savior. The Muslims marveled at the sacrificial love Isabella, Ava, and other Christians showed them by merely by taking the risk to go there and share the love of Christ with them. They deeply appreciated the sacrifice it took for Christians to leave their safe, comfortable homes and go to such a dangerous place and share in the suffering of so many Muslims. The Muslims who accepted Jesus expressed their desire to follow the God of the Bible that transforms His followers to love like that.

The above stories illustrate the following four next steps you can do as an individual, organization, or church.

First Next Step, Always!

The first step is to have a close, personal relationship with God. That is the first primary purpose God has for you and me. If you already have that, fantastic! If you do not yet have a growing and intimate relationship with God, make that your priority.

A close relationship with God is an essence of paradise. Before humankind sinned, they lived in paradise, marked by an intimate and harmonious relationship with God. When Jesus returns, paradise will be restored, and that relationship with God will be restored fully. The closer your relationship with God, the more spiritual paradise you will experience right now. And you will be fulfilling God's primary purpose for your life.

In the Bible, God tells us that we become close to Him by abiding in Jesus. We do that through daily Bible study and by praying that the Holy Spirit will help us understand more fully what we are studying in the Bible. Obey daily what God is revealing to you through the study of His word.

Through the above process, and in specific prayer for wisdom and direction, God will reveal your next steps to fulfilling His second primary purpose for your life: to be fruitful and multiply. Diligent prayer is wise and necessary for understanding your specific role in solving our true Islamic problem. We cannot change the world without God's help and guidance, and prayer is one powerful way we seek His wisdom and will. I also recommend adding fasting to the praying. For example, I often fast from eating any sweets for a month while I pray. My wife forgoes social media when we are seeking specific answers from God. Remember that when you seek His will and His kingdom, God will give you wisdom and answers.

This was the process for Roger in this chapter, as it was for me before the creation of iHOPE Ministries: abide in Jesus through deepening your knowledge of Him and seeking Him in daily prayer.

With iHOPE Ministries, believers like Roger can become a prayer partner with iPray. This is one of the most valuable things you can do as an iHOPE partner.

First Next Step as an Organization/Church

I will assume your church or organization is already seeking after God. With that in mind, regarding the role of your organization/church, you can begin by forming a team of leaders and/or influencers to diligently pray about how God can best use you. Some churches have formed small groups within the church that meet once a month after a church service to pray for individuals and ministries with whom they partner.

Second Next Step

As an individual, get adequately informed and equipped like Roger did so you can create an action plan and follow through with the Muslims you encounter. As an organization or a church, you can follow the example of Roger's church. You, too, can have a *glocal* impact.

Third Next Step

You can be part of God's mission by financially giving to individuals or ministries like iHOPE just like Roger did as an individual or like his church/organization. After individuals experience iHOPE training, some go on short-term trips like Isabella did. Isabella had dozens of others donate toward her trip. Each person who contributed to help her make that trip participated in the harvest God produced through Isabella.

Ava went to serve long-term in an Islamic area. She has more than one hundred individuals supporting her through ongoing prayers and encouragement and dozens who are supporting her financially so she can serve full-time. Ava's supporters, too, are part of the harvest God has and is producing through her. Every gift is important; none is too small or too large. The harvest truly is plentiful, and your financial partnership will help expand the solution to help change the world for future generations. Your financial resources can result in eternal fruit.

Regarding the sharing of the gospel, Romans 10:15 (NLT) says, "And how will anyone go and tell without being sent?" That is why the scriptures say, "How beautiful are the feet of messengers who bring good news!"

Fourth Next Step

Go!

Go and fulfill God's second primary purpose for your life by being fruitful and multiplying.

Go be His ambassador with the message of reconciliation God entrusted with us.

Go so God will redeem others through you.

Go make disciples.

Go be His witnesses.

Go locally like Roger and TCC leaders/congregants did with Muslims God sent to their area.

Go glocally like Roger did as an online ambassador.
Go globally on short-term trips like Isabella and Roger did.
Go globally long term and full time like Ava did.

Fourth Next Step as a Church/Organization

If your church/organization does not already have an evangelistic partner in an Islamic nation, I urge you to pray about getting one.

If you do not already have a partnership with a sending organization that works in Islamic nations, again, I urge you to pray about getting one. You can help increase the number of people who are reaching out to the unengaged and unreached peoples in Islamic areas of the world.

But how can they call on him to save them unless they believe in him? And how can they believe in him if they have never heard about him? And how can they hear about him unless someone tells them? And how will anyone go and tell them without being sent? (Romans 10:14–15a NLT)

God's Third Primary Purpose for Your Life

Before the fall, God gave three primary purposes for life. We have covered the first two. The third is found in Genesis 1:28 (NLT): "And govern it." And Genesis 2:15 (ESV): "In the garden of Eden to work it and keep it."

God gave us the most blessed opportunity, privilege, and responsibility to take care of His creation. As the rest of the Bible makes abundantly clear, God expects you and me to work diligently and faithfully in the areas of our God-given talents and abilities. Whatever your job, work it with integrity as God's representative in your workplace. By doing so, you are fulfilling God's third primary purpose for your life.

I hope it is clear by now that this book is not suggesting you must be in full-time ministry to fulfill God's second primary purpose for your life. The following short story illustrates this very well.

Pierre is in full-time ministry. He travels regularly to Islamic areas to work with evangelistic partners who share Christ with Muslims. Elias is a highly successful businessperson and is Pierre's biggest financial supporter. Elias was considering leaving his thriving business to serve in full-time ministry alongside Pierre.

In preparation for full-time ministry, Elias spent a year doing many of the things Pierre does, including going on several short-term trips to Islamic areas. In summary, Elias's ministry work did not go well. Toward the end, Elias made a statement that sounded like the following: "It takes me about two weeks of challenging work and much stress to accomplish badly what Pierre achieves with excellence in one day." Interestingly, Elias and Pierre agreed that the reverse was true. When Pierre tried to handle some of Elias's business responsibilities, he could not do well what Elias did so well.

With that in mind, after fasting and praying, Elias realized God had gifted him well for his work. His wisest course of action, then, was to continue working his business for God's glory. Elias focuses on excelling in his work and earning money so he can give a generous percentage of it to support gospel-centered ministries like iHOPE and individuals like Pierre.

Elias is fulfilling God's three primary purposes. He is intentional about knowing God and about being fruitful and multiplying. He encourages, prays, and financially supports Pierre, iHOPE, and others through whom God is producing abundant harvests.

Elias, meanwhile, also looks for opportunities to do the five essentials everywhere he goes. For example, Elias traveled on business to a major city in a Christianized nation. The taxi driver there was Muslim. Elias went on to share his Christian faith with him, prayed with him in the name of Jesus, loved on him by giving him a Bible, and offered to connect him with local Christians who could follow through with him.

Like Elias, you can fulfill God's three primary purposes for your life, whether in full-time ministry or not.

The Final Story

I hope this final story will encourage you as you seek God to reveal the role He has planned for you as you fulfill His primary purposes for your life. If you trust God and obey His will for you, it will be the best and most fulfilling thing you will ever do.

The years surrounding 2008 were the most challenging years of my life. And with the life I have experienced, that is saying a lot. I knew then that God had three primary purposes for the lives of each of his children. I accepted Jesus as my Savior, so I knew that I was saved. I felt secure that at least God's primary purpose of redeeming me for an eternal relationship with Him was achieved. But I did not yet have a close relationship with God. I attended church most weekends, but I prayed and read my Bible sporadically, and I knew I was not doing a good job fulfilling God's other primary purposes for my life. In other words, I had not surrendered my life to Jesus as Lord over all my actions.

Hitting Rock Bottom

Something was missing, but I wasn't sure exactly what it was, nor did I know what to do about it. For years, I did things I thought God wanted me to do, but I was not successful in anything. I failed in marriage, and I was bankrupt financially. I hit rock bottom in every area of my life. I thought that all the terrible things I was experiencing were the consequences I had earned because of my previous decades of sinful living apart from God.

I got a life-changing illness that does not have a medical cure. It seemed like I was physically falling apart. The chronic and severe pain I endured daily made me wonder if I would ever work again. Completely drained emotionally, I felt worthless in every area of life, including in ministry. I fasted and prayed, but I did not hear any answers from God. I pleaded with Him, often sobbing on my knees or lying flat on the ground, void of any strength. But God was silent. Nothing made sense to me.

All that led to me creating a detailed plan to end my life. It was planned to look accidental so I did not leave my family with any trauma related to me taking my own life. I told God that I could not take life on earth anymore, and I was coming home to be with Him. I was counting on His forgiveness for the sin of utter weakness that I was about to commit.

But God ...

God spoke to me. First, it was not with words, but with His actions. You see, for one week I repeatedly tried plan A to end my life, but God intervened miraculously, and I failed. It was clear to me that it was God at work. I responded with anger at God because I just wanted to die. Stubbornly I went with plan B, a plan I thought would require a greater miracle to stop.

But God stopped that one as well. I got even angrier at God, screaming at Him, then sobbing. I kept crying until it appeared I had no more tears left in me. I just kept telling God that I had nothing left in me, that I felt so weak in every area. I told God, "I tried to do things for You, but I failed. Now that I am penniless and with a body that is unhealthy and falling apart, I just want to go home."

Then God spoke, this time audibly. It was the first time I ever heard God speak. It was a firm voice in my head. God said several things to me. Some, if not all, apply to you.

For When You Are Weak, Then You Are Strong

The first thing God told me was, "My grace is all you need. My power works best in weakness."

I recognized that God had shared 2 Corinthians 12:9 with me.

Through His word, God taught me that His grace is bigger than my sins, and His strength infinitely greater than my weakness.

As I sat quietly processing that personal encounter with Him, God spoke again.

You Are the Light of the World

"Look up."

It was night, and I was by a window. I looked outside, thinking perhaps God wanted me to look outside and into the sky, but I only saw a dark, black sky. God kept telling me to look, and as I looked more intently and focused more, I could see some stars twinkling in the distance. The more I looked, the more stars I saw filling the night sky. The stars went from twinkling to sparkling, brightening the night sky.

God taught me that evening that we typically do not seek more light when we are living in bright times of our lives. But when we are going through dark times in our lives, only then do we seek light. It is then that, if we look intently, we will see God shining through the darkness.

This message from God applies to you and me right now. God states in Matthew 5:14–16 (NIV), "You are the light of the world ... Let your light shine before others."

God's light is shining through us as believers in Jesus Christ. God entrusted us with His light. Around 1.43 billion Muslims worldwide, both locally and globally, need every Christian (you and me) to come close to them to let the light of Christ shine through us for them to see.

We are not to be afraid of the darkness; rather, Jesus commanded us to go into the dark world and allow God's light to shine through us to illuminate the darkness. Too often we have submitted to fear or hatred and hidden the light of Christ away from those 1.43 billion Muslims. It will take every Christian uncovering their light to pierce the darkness.

When Christians have acted as instruments of God's light, as they did so brilliantly in the first six hundred years after Christ's ascension,

God's light illuminated the darkness. But since the birth of Islam, Christians have, for the most part, kept the light away from Muslims. We are covering the light, and the darkness is spreading.

God called me that night and is calling you right now to get up and rely on Him—to rely on His grace and strength. Let's go and illuminate the darkness with His light uncovered and shining through us to make this a better world today and for future generations.

You Are the Salt of the Earth

That night God continued His message to me, and it applies to you today. He reminded me of Jesus's words in Matthew 5:13 (NIV): "You are the salt of the earth."

Typically, in preparation for usage, salt is gathered. As a Christian, you are prepared for use through gatherings in church, worship, prayer, and Bible study. These gatherings and churches are like the saltshaker.

But salt does not do its intended job if it remains in the saltshaker. Salt is essential for life, but it needs to spread properly—outside of the container. Salt is a purifying and preserving agent. Jesus gives us the most blessed opportunity and responsibility to be this soul-saving agent with Muslims. God is sending Muslims to your area so you can be salt among them, planting seeds of the good news of Jesus so they may be saved. Only with the proper usage of salt outside the shaker can salt help purify and preserve life.

World Changers

When I surrendered to God, He enabled me with His grace, strength, light, and love to take the next steps in life and ministry. God put my life back together. As I faithfully trusted and obeyed God, He gave me the step-by-step guidance for the journey to fulfill His primary purposes for the lives of each of His children.

I believe God handpicked you to read this book. He is inviting you to join the movement and to invite your church, organization, and friends to know Him and make Him known among Muslims everywhere. Together we can be world changers and make the future brighter for generations to come.

Names and locations have been changed to protect the identities of the people

Printed in the United States
By Bookmasters